love your
library

Buckinghamshire Libraries

Search, renew or reserve online 24/7
www.buckscc.gov.uk/libraries

24 hour renewal line
0303 123 0035

Enquiries
01296 382415

follow us **twitter**

@Bucks_Libraries

CONTENTS

ISTANBUL

Few of the world's cities capture the imagination quite like Istanbul, superbly situated at the confluence of predominantly Christian Europe and the largely Muslim Middle East. It is a booming megalopolis of more than fifteen million people, standing astride both the Asian and European sides of the Bosphorus strait, the vibrant cultural and economic powerhouse of a resurgent Turkish Republic. Of course, Istanbul has been a major city for over two thousand years, and it is the incredible legacy of the two great empires which made it their capital, the Christian Byzantines and Muslim Ottoman Turks, that make it so appealing today.

Rüstem Paşa Camii

A perfect kebab

For most visitors, Istanbul is a city of two, albeit rather uneven, halves. The first is the old city, strategically located on a peninsula pointing east across the Bosphorus towards Asia, and cut-off from the European mainland to the west by the substantial remains of the monumental Byzantine-era land walls. The peninsula is bound to the south by the glimmering waters of the Sea of Marmara, to the north by the curving inlet of one of the world's finest natural harbours, the Golden Horn. Like ancient Rome, which Constantinople superseded as the Roman Empire's major city, it was built on seven hills. There is so much to see and do in the old city that you could spend weeks exploring its many sights, but even with just a few days at your disposal it's possible to get a real flavour of this great metropolis. Fortunately, the majority of the major sights, such as the Haghia Sophia (Aya Sofya), Topkapı Palace and Blue Mosque, are located within a short distance of each other in compact Sultanahmet.

Best places for a perfect kebab

Forget that soggy late-night kebab at your local takeaway. Real kebabs come in many forms in the land of their birth and eating them is a seriously enjoyable business. Try a metre-long special at *Akdeniz Hatay Sofrası* (see page 70), a lunchtime stand-up treat at *Dönerci Şahin Üsta* (see page 69), a southeast Turkish delight at *Develi* (see page 83) or a *rakı*-enhanced kebab feast at *Kenan Üsta Ocakbaşı* (see page 107).

The second half of the city is the European quarter of Beyoğlu and Galata, north across the Golden Horn from the old city and easily reached by tram or metro. As well as being home to the famous Galata Tower and a host of wonderful, mainly nineteenth-century buildings, it is Istanbul's entertainment hub. Even if you've no interest in the hedonistic delights of cinema-going, gallery-gazing, shopping, bar-hopping, puffing on a water pipe or clubbing, you should come here to challenge your preconceptions of what a predominantly Muslim city is like, dine at one of the myriad (usually excellent) restaurants or simply join the Friday or Saturday crush of people surging down İstiklal Caddesi. Then, if there's time, a bargain ferry ride to Asia awaits.

Young people drinking and dining out in a backstreet of Tünel

By far the best way to explore is on foot, especially as there are so many smaller, easily missed sights tucked-in between the major ones, from Byzantine cisterns to historic Turkish baths. The buzzing waterfront around the Golden Horn-spanning Galata Bridge is unmissable, and offers superb views up to the old city's exotic skyline of domes and slender minarets. Try, too, to get a taste of the conservative parts of the old city by walking a section of the land walls or exploring the backstreets of the northwest quarter. Although the language barrier may be formidable and street signage less than perfect, don't be afraid to wander off the beaten path and temporarily mislay yourself. After all, with water on three sides and the towering land walls on the fourth you'll eventually reach an unmissable landmark.

When to visit

Hot, humid summers and cold, damp winters mean spring and autumn are the best times to visit, with May–June and September–October offering the (usually) dry, warm weather ideal for exploring on foot. Needless to say, this is also the most expensive time for accommodation. Midsummer is more than bearable, however, with maximum temperatures rarely exceeding 28 degrees – avoid long tramps during the hottest part of the day and enjoy the benefits of warm evenings in a rooftop bar or restaurant. One downside of midsummer visits is that many Istanbulites decamp to Aegean resorts and some clubs close for the duration. Winters can be snowy, most likely in January or February, or more usually simply cold, wet and windy (the downside of the city's proximity to so much water means it has a maritime climate). Fog can also be a problem in winter, sometimes closing the Bosphorus to shipping. On the plus side, hotel rates are cheaper and the arts and cultural scene vibrant.

Where to...
Shop

With some four thousand shops in a mall over five hundred years old, the **Grand Bazaar** is a shopping experience few visitors will want to miss. There's everything from fake designer jeans to centuries-old Turkish rugs and plenty of cafés to take the weight off your feet for a while. The **Spice Bazaar** in Eminönü is more manageable and equally historic, while the streets around it are wonderful for foodstuffs. The **Arasta Bazaar** near the Blue Mosque is good for quality Turkish souvenirs; for more food shopping, head to **Kadıköy** in Asia or into conservative Fatih for the Çarşamba Pazarı (Wednesday Bazaar). For fashion, try **İstiklal Caddesi**.
OUR FAVOURITES: Istanbul Handicrafts Centre see page 55, Safa see page 55, Historia Mall see page 68

Drink

Turkey may be predominantly Muslim but there are plenty of places to enjoy a drink in Istanbul. The most lively area by far is buzzing **Galata/Beyoğlu**, where student bars rub shoulders with hip licensed cafés and the well-heeled sip cocktails at expensive rooftop establishments. **Nevizade Sokak** in Beyoğlu is particularly noted for its raucous drinking (and eating) scene, particularly madcap on a Friday and Saturday night. The old city is much quieter, though there are plenty of places on Divan Yolu and Akbıyık Caddesi for a beer, glass of wine or the national drink, *rakı*, an aniseed spirit.
OUR FAVOURITES: Istanbul Terrace Bar see page 41, Fes Cafe see page 69, Mila see page 125

Eat

Istanbulites are fussy and demanding when it comes to food. Whether choosing a humble *simit* (sesame-coated bread ring) from a street barrow or a freshly caught fish in a stylish Bosphorus-front restaurant, they'll only accept the best. Fish is highly prized, but more regular foods include all kinds of *sulu yemek* (stews), served-up from big steamtrays, the Turkish "pizzas" *pide* and *lahmacun*, a bewildering array of savoury pies and breads, soups and, inevitably, kebabs – either grilled on skewers over charcoal at an *ocakbaşı* or sliced from a rotating spit at a *dönerci*. However tempting for ease, don't just dine in tourist-dominated Sultanahmet, head across to **Galata/Beyoğlu**, further west in the old city – or across to **Asia**.
OUR FAVOURITES: Asitane see page 83, Nola Galata see page 92, Mikla see page 107

Go Out

The old city has very little in the way of genuine nightlife. The real action is across the Golden Horn, primarily in and around **İstiklal Caddesi** in **Beyoğlu**, where there are clubs catering to every taste, from hard rock to dance and jazz to blues. **Galata** has a few small bohemian venues, as does **Kadıköy** in Asia. For pop glitz, head down to the Bosphorus-front in Ortaköy/Kuruçeşme. For something more Turkish, try a *meyhane*, a kind of tavern, where the food (usually fish) takes second place to drink and the locals sing and dance to traditional Turkish music, as in **Kumkapı** in the old city.
OUR FAVOURITES: Just Bar see page 41, Fosil see page 93, Limoncello see page 117

Istanbul at a glance

Galata and the waterfront districts p.84.
Up-and-coming bohemian quarter famed for its landmark tower and fabulous views to the old city.

HASKÖY

GAL

KASİMPAŞA

GOLDEN HORN

GALAT

Northwest quarter and the land walls p.72.
Wander the atmospheric backstreets of the city's most conservative quarter, or along the six kilometres of the most successful fortification ever built.

FATİH

ZEYREK

SÜLEYMANIYE

AKSARAY

KUMKAPI

Grand Bazaar District p.58.
A fascinating quarter centred on a sprawling fifteenth-century shopping mall and sublime hilltop mosque.

Sultanahmet p.24.
The heart of the historic old ideal for exploring on foot.

0	metres	500
0	yards	500

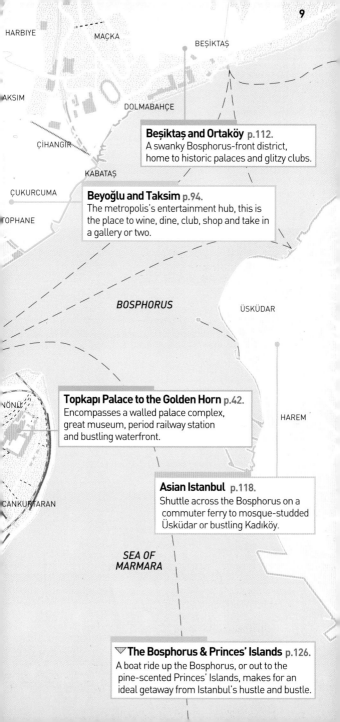

HARBIYE

MAÇKA

BEŞİKTAŞ

DOLMABAHÇE

AKSIM

ÇIHANGIR

KABATAŞ

ÇUKURCUMA

TOPHANE

Beşiktaş and Ortaköy p.112.
A swanky Bosphorus-front district,
home to historic palaces and glitzy clubs.

Beyoğlu and Taksim p.94.
The metropolis's entertainment hub, this is
the place to wine, dine, club, shop and take in
a gallery or two.

BOSPHORUS

ÜSKÜDAR

NÖNÜ

Topkapı Palace to the Golden Horn p.42.
Encompasses a walled palace complex,
great museum, period railway station
and bustling waterfront.

HAREM

CANKURTARAN

Asian Istanbul p.118.
Shuttle across the Bosphorus on a
commuter ferry to mosque-studded
Üsküdar or bustling Kadıköy.

*SEA OF
MARMARA*

▽ **The Bosphorus & Princes' Islands** p.126.
A boat ride up the Bosphorus, or out to the
pine-scented Princes' Islands, makes for an
ideal getaway from Istanbul's hustle and bustle.

15

Things not to miss

It's not really possible to see everything that Istanbul has to offer in one trip – and we don't suggest you try. What follows is a selective taste of their highlights – from fantastic architecture to charming markets.

< **Mosaic Museum Büyük**
See page 31
Charming collection of mosaics from the long-gone Byzantine Great Palace.

∨ **Church of the Pammakaristos**
See page 76
A typical late Byzantine church-turned-mosque adorned with stunning mosaics.

< **Haghia Sophia**
See page 25
The most important church of the Byzantine world was converted into a mosque in 1453, and a museum in 1934.

∨ **Istanbul Modern**
See page 94
The name says it all, a real contrast to the sights of the old city.

∧ Grand Bazaar
See page 59
This fifteenth-century covered market boasts 66 streets and over 4000 shops – the ultimate mall.

< Ayasofya Hürrem
See page 30
Ottoman hamams were temples to hygiene, godliness and gossip.

∧ **Galata Tower**
See page 84
Gaze across the busy waters of the Golden Horn to the exotic skyline of the old city.

∨ **360 bar-restaurant**
See page 108
This swanky rooftop establishment delivers what its name promises – at a price.

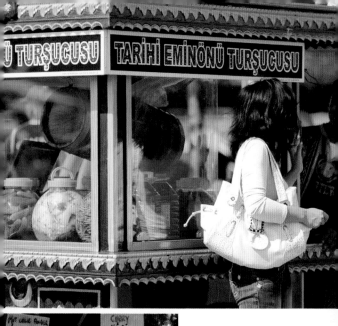

∧ Street cart snacks
See page 24
Sesame-coated bagels, roast chestnuts and sweetcorn are among the goodies pushed around Sultanahmet's streets.

< Spice Bazaar
See page 52
A centuries-old waterfront bazaar packed with spices, herbs and Turkish delight.

< **İstiklal Caddesi**
See page 94
High-street shops, historic arcades, a mall and much more.

∨ **Bosphorus cruise**
See page 126
A bargain ferry ride up the continent-dividing Bosphorus strait is a great day out.

THINGS NOT TO MISS

Day One in Istanbul

Haghia Sophia. See page 25. The mosaic-clad interior of the domed Haghia Sophia (Aya Sofya), for a thousand years the largest enclosed space in the world, still impresses today.

Basilica Cistern. See page 24. Beautifully lit and atmospheric underground Byzantine cistern, famed for its Medusa-head carvings and lazy carp.

Lunch. See page 38. Grilled meatballs are a Turkish favourite, and *Tarihi Sultanahmet Köftecisi*, overlooking the heart of the old city, does them to perfection.

Blue Mosque. See page 34. With its cascade of domes and plethora of gorgeous blue tiles from which its name derives, the Blue Mosque is unmissable.

Hippodrome. See page 33. A relatively tranquil square, this was in Roman and Byzantine times a chariot-racing circuit, dominated by the splendid Egyptian Obelisk.

Sokollu Mehmet Paşa Camii. See page 32. A beautiful Ottoman mosque tucked away in the backstreets near the Hippodrome.

Church of St Sergius and Bacchus. See page 31. Below the Hippodrome, this former early-Byzantine church is today the Little Haghia Sophia (Küçük Aya Sofya Camii), a working mosque.

Dinner. See page 40. Sample a multitude of delicious cold and hot *meze* morsels (starters) at *Giritli* before a fish main, washed down, if you you go for the fixed-meal deal, with an unlimited amount of wine, *rakı* or beer.

Haghia Sophia

Basilica Cistern

Giritli

Day Two in Istanbul

Topkapı Palace. See page 43. Make an early start to explore this fascinating palace complex, ranged around a series of attractive courtyard gardens.

Archeology Museum. See page 42. Receiving far less attention than it deserves, this fine museum exhibits a wealth of artefacts from the former Ottoman domains.

🍽 **Lunch**. See page 56. Grab a fish sandwich from *Tarihi Eminönü Balık Ekmek* and enjoy the vibrant chaos of Eminönü waterfront.

Spice Bazaar. See page 52. Admire the beautifully arranged spices for sale in this covered Ottoman market – but make your purchases in the streets round about.

Rüstem Paşa Camii. See page 54. A gem of a mosque in the bustling bazaar quarter of Eminönü, noted for its gorgeous İznik tiles.

☕ **Coffee**. See page 68. After toiling up the third hill, stop in the "hidden" *Ağa Kapısı* café for incomparable views down to the Galata Bridge and Bosphorus.

Süleymaniye Külliyesi. See page 58. This mosque complex is the masterwork of the Ottomans' greatest architect – unmissable.

Süleymaniye Hamamı. See page 59. Part of the mosque complex; unwind after your heavy day in this steamy and attractive hamam.

🍽 **Dinner**. See page 40. For kebabs made with various meats, *Şirvan Sofrasi*, a popular place in the Sultanahmet district, is perfect.

Topkapı Palace

Archeology Museum

Spice Bazaar

Backstreet Istanbul

The biggest and best concentration of traditional backstreets is in the conservative northwest quarter. Winding their way along the old city's fourth, fifth and sixth hills, they are home to many seldom-visited sights and afford great views.

Aqueduct of Valens. See page 66. You can't miss the two-tiered arches of this Byzantine engineering marvel spanning traffic-clogged Atatürk Bulvarı.

Yavuz Selim Camii. See page 75. Beautifully austere imperial mosque atop the old city's fifth hill, offering grand views over the Golden Horn.

Church of the Pammakaristos. See page 76. The funerary chapel of this little-visited Byzantine jewel is today a museum with some fine mosaics.

Aqueduct of Valens

🍴 **Lunch**. See page 83. Noted for updated versions of traditional Ottoman dishes, *Asitane* is right next to the Kariye Museum.

The Kariye Museum. See page 72. Every picture tells a story at the former Church of St Saviour in Chora, one of the best collections of Byzantine mosaics anywhere.

The land walls. See page 79. Follow the mighty land walls down to the Golden Horn, past the once-grand Palace of the Porphyrogenitus.

Ferry to Asia. See page 147. A ferry from the jetty at Ayvansaray runs down the Horn and across the Bosphorus to Üsküdar.

🍴 **Dinner**. See page 125. Eat at *Kanaat Lokantası*, a very traditional (and dry) restaurant in conservative Üsküdar.

Asitane

The Kariye Museum

The European quarter

The old city may have all the major historic sights, but for a hint of fin-de-siècle decadence, a generous slice of the contemporary arts and a no-holds-barred night on the town, try the European quarter.

Istanbul Modern. See page 94. Great introduction to modern Turkish art and plenty of temporary exhibitions at this Bosphorus-front retort to London's Tate Modern.

Galata Tower. See page 84. Ascend to the balcony of this landmark Genoese tower for superb vistas.

Lunch. See page 91. The views from the popular rooftop *Galata Konak* café-cum-patisserie are just wonderful.

Galata Mevlevi Lodge. See page 84. See the hall where the dervishes whirled in this fascinating little museum.

İstiklal Caddesi. See page 94. Formerly the Grand Rue de Pera and lined with fine nineteenth-century buildings, this is the city's premier shopping and entertainment street.

Tea. See page 98. The tearooms of the grand *Pera Palace Hotel* are a period delight.

Pera Museum. See page 98. Fine gallery-cum-museum housed in a beautifully restored nineteenth-century building.

Dinner. See page 106. A lively Istanbul-Greek *meyhane* (taverna), *İmroz* is great for a raucous meal out.

Venue. See page 93. *Nardis Jazz Club*, a short hop from the Galata Tower, is a cool and sophisticated venue.

View of the Golden Horn from Galata Tower

İstiklal Caddesi

Tea at the Kubbeli Saloon Lounge, Pera Palace Hotel

PLACES

Praying at the Blue Mosque

Sultanahmet

Once the fulcrum of both the Christian Byzantine and Muslim Ottoman empires, Sultanahmet is the heart of old Istanbul. The essence of its grand, imperial past is distilled in two truly great, domed buildings facing each other imperiously over an attractive park – the monumental sixth-century church of Haghia Sophia, today the Aya Sofya Museum, and the equally impressive Blue Mosque, built a thousand years later. There are plenty more notable, historic buildings scattered across the crown of the peninsula and in the old alleys running down to the shipping-filled blue waters of the Sea of Marmara, and you could easily spend two or three days sightseeing in Sultanahmet alone. Inevitably, tourism is Sultanahmet's raison d'être today, and there are legions of hotels, cafés and restaurants catering to visitors' needs.

Milion

MAP P.26, POCKET MAP H11
Divan Yolu ⊕ 1 Sultanahmet.

Unfortunately, most visitors, in their rush to get to the nearby Haghia Sophia, walk by the remains of the Milion without noticing it – hardly surprising, given that it is a mere stump of marble lost in a verge at the eastern end of busy Divan Yolu. This is all that's left of the Milion, a once-magnificent **triumphal arch** surmounted by a cross, flanked on either side by a statue of the Emperor Constantine and his mother Helena, beneath which was a milestone measuring distances to all corners of the Roman Empire. The crudely built stone tower next to it is actually an Ottoman-era water regulator for the Basilica Cistern (Yerebatan Sarnıcı) below your feet.

Basilica Cistern (Yerebatan Sarnıcı)

MAP P.26, POCKET MAP H11
Yerebatan Cad 1/3 ⊕ 1 Sultanahmet ⊕ 0212 512 1570, ⊛ yerebatan.com. Daily 9am–5.30pm. ₺20, audio-guide ₺15.

The Yerebatan Sarnıcı or "Sunken Cistern", just downhill from the Milion, is better known to foreigners as the Basilica Cistern. Reached by a long flight of stairs and atmospherically lit, it proves a major hit with most visitors. Built originally under Emperor Constantine when he was refounding the city as his new imperial capital, it was much modified in the sixth century. It could hold up to 80,000 cubic metres of water, used to supply the Great Palace of Byzantine-era Constantinople and, in the Ottoman period, the Topkapı Palace. The attractive roof, comprising a series of brick-built domes, is supported by a veritable forest of 336 columns arranged in 12 rows of 28, each topped by a capital, the most attractive of which are of the elaborately carved, acanthus-leaf Corinthian variety. Walkways lead through the columns, allowing visitors to admire the carp swimming in the shallow, clear and subtly illuminated waters, as well as wonder at the massive amount of work its 1987 restoration must have been, when some 50,000 tonnes of mud were dredged out of the 140m long by 70m wide cistern. At the far end of the cistern are two massive capitals, both carved into the form of the snake-haired mythological creature **Medusa** and each supporting a pillar. Almost certainly reused from much earlier structures, one Medusa is upside down, the other laid on its side, possibly because the Medusa was a pagan symbol and the cistern was built in the Christian period. A scene from the 1963 James Bond film *From Russia with Love* was shot here.

Cafer Ağa Theological School (Cafer Ağa Mecresesi)

MAP P.26, POCKET MAP H11

Caferiye Sok ⊕ 1 Sultanahmet ⊕ 0212 513 3601. Tues–Sun 9.30am–6pm.

In the shadow of the Haghia Sophia, this former Islamic theological school was designed by the prolific Ottoman master architect Sinan in the sixteenth century. The domed rooms ranged around the attractive courtyard, formerly the cells of the theology students, are now home to the studios of craftspeople maintaining traditional Ottoman arts such as *ebru* (marbling), calligraphy and the painting of miniatures. Many of their wares are for sale and the whole enterprise is surprisingly low-key given that it is situated in the most heavily touristed part of the city.

Haghia Sophia (Aya Sofya)

MAP P.26, POCKET MAP H11

Sultanahmet Meydanı 1 ⊕ 1 Sultanahmet ⊕ 0212 522 1750, ⓦ ayasofyamuzesi.gov. tr. Tues–Sun: mid-April–Oct 9am–7pm, last entry 6pm; Nov–mid-April 9am–5pm, last entry 4pm. ₺60, audio-guide ₺20.

Representative of the Byzantine Empire at the peak of its power in the sixth century, the Haghia Sophia, or **Church of the Holy Wisdom**, still inspires awe today. Two previous churches of the same name had stood on the site before being razed, the latter in a riot in 532. Justinian, determined to bolster his

Basilica Cistern

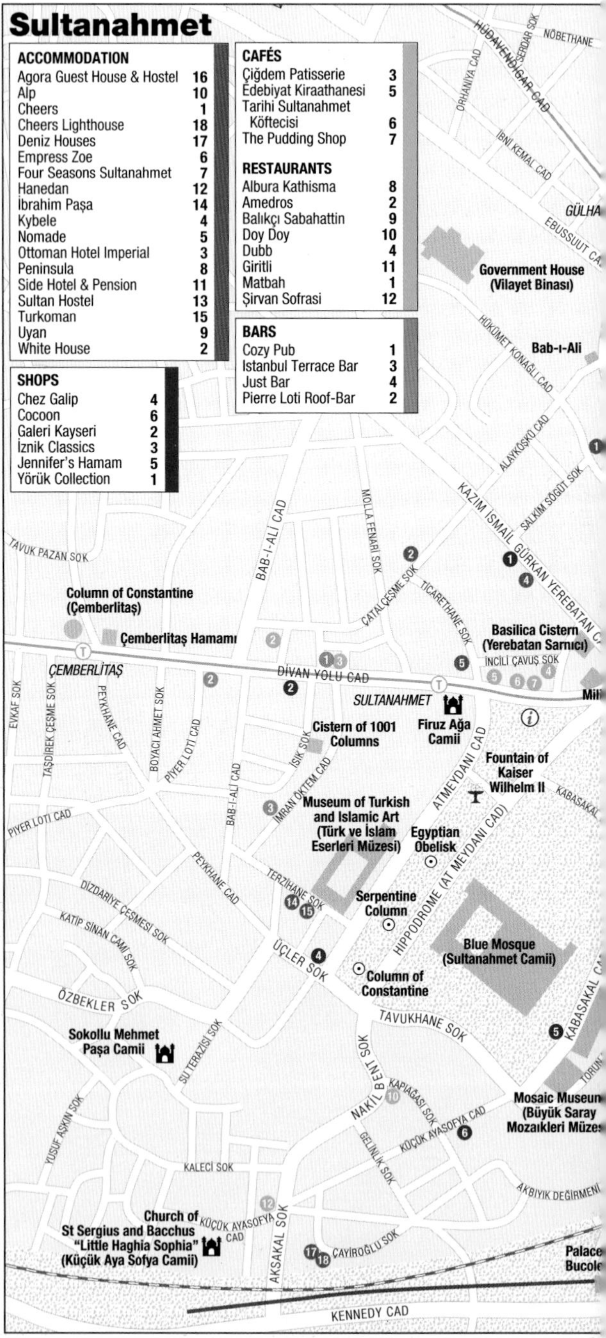

Sultanahmet
ACCOMMODATION
Agora Guest House & Hostel 16
Alp 10
Cheers 1
Cheers Lighthouse 18
Deniz Houses 17
Empress Zoe 6
Four Seasons Sultanahmet 7
Hanedan 12
İbrahim Paşa 14
Kybele 4
Nomade 5
Ottoman Hotel Imperial 3
Peninsula 8
Side Hotel & Pension 11
Sultan Hostel 13
Turkoman 15
Uyan 9
White House 2
SHOPS
Chez Galip 4
Cocoon 6
Galeri Kayseri 2
İznik Classics 3
Jennifer's Hamam 5
Yörük Collection 1
CAFÉS
Çiğdem Patisserie 3
Edebiyat Kiraathanesi 5
Tarihi Sultanahmet Köftecisi 6
The Pudding Shop 7
RESTAURANTS
Albura Kathisma 8
Amedros 2
Balıkçı Sabahattin 9
Doy Doy 10
Dubb 4
Giritli 11
Matbah 1
Şirvan Sofrasi 12
BARS
Cozy Pub 1
Istanbul Terrace Bar 3
Just Bar 4
Pierre Loti Roof-Bar 2
HÜDAVENDİGAR CAD
SERDAR SOK
NÖBETHANE
ORHANIYA CAD
İBNİ KEMAL CAD
GÜLHA
EBUSSUUT CA
Government House (Vilayet Binası)
HÜKÜMET KONAĞI CAD
Bab-ı-Ali
ALAYKÖŞKÜ CAD
SALKIM SÖĞÜT SOK
KAZIM İSMAİL GÜRKAN YEREBATAN C
MOLLA FENARİ SOK
BAB-I-ALİ CAD
TAVUK PAZAN SOK
ÇATALÇEŞME SOK
TİCARETHANE SOK
Column of Constantine (Çemberlitaş)
Çemberlitaş Hamamı
Basilica Cistern (Yerebatan Sarnıcı)
İNCİLİ ÇAVUŞ SOK
ÇEMBERLİTAŞ
DİVAN YOLU CAD
SULTANAHMET
Mili
EVKAF SOK
TAŞDİREK ÇEŞME SOK
PEYKHANE CAD
BOYACI AHMET SOK
PİYER LOTİ CAD
IŞIK SOK
Cistern of 1001 Columns
Firuz Ağa Camii
ATMEYDANI CAD
Fountain of Kaiser Wilhelm II
KABASAKAL
İMRAN ÖKTEM CAD
Museum of Turkish and Islamic Art (Türk ve İslam Eserleri Müzesi)
Egyptian Obelisk
HIPPODROME (AT MEYDANI CAD)
PİYER LOTİ CAD
PEYKHANE CAD
TERZİHANE SOK
DİZDARİYE ÇEŞMESİ SOK
KATİP SİNAN CAMİ SOK
Serpentine Column
Blue Mosque (Sultanahmet Camii)
ÜÇLER SOK
Column of Constantine
ÖZBEKLER SOK
TAVUKHANE SOK
KABASAKAL C
Sokollu Mehmet Paşa Camii
SU TERAZİSİ SOK
NAKİL BENT SOK
KAPIAĞASI SOK
TORUN
Mosaic Museum (Büyük Saray Mozaikleri Müzesi)
YUSUF AŞKIN SOK
GELİNLİK SOK
KÜÇÜK AYASOFYA CAD
KALECİ SOK
AKBIYIK DEĞİRMENİ
Church of St Sergius and Bacchus "Little Haghia Sophia" (Küçük Aya Sofya Camii)
KÜÇÜK AYASOFYA CAD
AKSAKAL SOK
ÇAYIROĞLU SOK
Palace Bucole
KENNEDY CAD

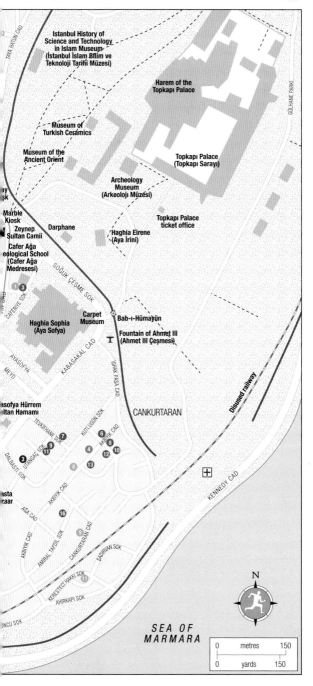

Istanbul History of
Science and Technology
in Islam Museum
(İstanbul İslam Bilim ve
Teknoloji Tarihi Müzesi)

Harem of the
Topkapı Palace

Museum of
Turkish Ceramics

Museum of the
Ancient Orient

Topkapı Palace
(Topkapı Sarayı)

Archeology
Museum
(Arkeoloji Müzesi)

Marble
Kiosk

Zeynep
Sultan Camii

Darphane

Topkapı Palace
ticket office

Cafer Ağa
eological School
(Cafer Ağa
Medresesi)

Haghia Eirene
(Aya İrini)

SOĞUK ÇEŞME SOK

CAFERİYE SOK

Carpet
Museum

Bab-ı-Hümayün

Haghia Sophia
(Aya Sofya)

Fountain of Ahmet III
(Ahmet III Çeşmesi)

KABASAKAL CAD

İSHAK PAŞA CAD

AYASOFYA

MEYD

sofya Hürrem
Itan Hamamı

CANKURTARAN

TEVKİFHANE SOK

KUTLUGUN SOK

AKBIYIK CAD

DALBASTI SOK

UTANGAÇ SOK

AKBIYIK CAD

Disused railway

KENNEDY CAD

sta
aar

AĞA CAD

AKBIYIK CAD

AMİRAL TAFDİL SOK

CANKURTARAN CAD

ŞADIRVAN SOK

KERESTECİ HAKKI SOK

AHIRKAPI SOK

UNCU SOK

TAYA HATUN CAD

GÜLHANE PARKI

*SEA OF
MARMARA*

N

| 0 | metres | 150 |
| 0 | yards | 150 |

Haghia Sophia interior

temporal and spiritual authority, ordered a rebuild on a scale not realized before. The architects, Greek mathematician Anthemius and geometer Isidore, came up with an innovative and much-imitated design – covering a near-square building with a dome of unprecedented height and impressive diameter.

Sunk a few metres below current ground-level at the entrance to Justinian's masterpiece is the stepped base of the second church, along with a series of blocks which once adorned its facade, relief-carved with sheep symbolizing the Twelve Apostles. The so-called "Beautiful Gate", the central door of five, leads to the **inner narthex**, a vaulted vestibule containing the sarcophagus of the Empress Irene. Further doorways lead to the inner narthex, its ceiling glittering with gold mosaics and containing, above the imperial portal leading to the nave, a stunning mosaic panel depicting an all-powerful Christ being beseeched by Emperor Leo IV.

It is the **nave** of the church, however, that is truly inspiring.

Here the 32m-diameter central dome, towering 55m above floor level, appears to be suspended in mid-air, its supporting piers cleverly concealed in the twin line of pillars separating the nave from the aisles. Two half-domes join the central dome to the west and east, emphasizing the sense of space, an effect aided by light filtering in from the forty windows puncturing the dome. Also on the ground floor is the **weeping column**, so-called because it "sweats" water and supposedly cures all ills, and the omphalos, a marble-inlay floor panel where coronations took place.

Following the 1453 Ottoman Turkish conquest of the city, this church became, as the **Aya Sofya Camii**, the city's major mosque. Thus the apse is pierced by a Mecca-facing niche (*mihrab*), flanked to one side by a prayer-platform (*mimber*). There's also the loge, a platform used by the Sultan at Friday prayers, and eight large plaques below the dome adorned with Arabic calligraphy. Outside, the four minarets at each corner of the building were added post-Ottoman conquest. It was turned into the Aya Sofya museum in 1934.

Reached by a stone ramp from the inner narthex's north end are the **upper galleries**. The south gallery is the most interesting as it contains several beautifully executed and preserved Byzantine mosaic panels, including one depicting John the Baptist and the Virgin Mary beseeching an impassive-looking Christ to save humanity. Scratched into the marble balustrade here is some Viking graffiti, probably scrawled by a member of the Varangian Guard, bodyguards to the Byzantine emperors recruited from Scandinavia. Exiting via the south end of the inner narthex, in the **Vestibule of Warriors**, is the pick of the church's mosaic panels. Executed in the late tenth century, it depicts the Virgin and Child. On her right, Emperor Justinian offers a model of the Haghia Sophia church; to her left, an even more munificent Emperor Constantine presents her with a model of his city, Constantinople.

Soğuk Çeşme Sokağı

MAP P.26, POCKET MAP H11

🚏 1 Sultanahmet.

In Turkish, Soğuk Çeşme Sokağı means "street of the cold fountains", though the cobbled alley is notable today not for its fountains but for the attractively restored nineteenth-century wooden houses lining its cobbled course. It's worth strolling down this pedestrianized lane to see a version of how the old city would have looked before the modern era, when the then-standard wooden houses, subject to frequent fires, were rebuilt in brick and concrete. The houses are attractively painted, with traditional overhanging upper floors.

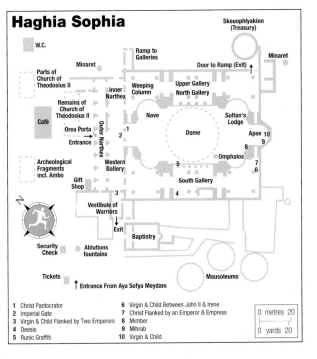

Haghia Sophia

1 Christ Pantocrator
2 Imperial Gate
3 Virgin & Child Flanked by Two Emperors
4 Deesis
5 Runic Graffiti

6 Virgin & Child Between John II & Irene
7 Christ Flanked by an Emperor & Empress
8 Mimber
9 Mihrab
10 Virgin & Child

0 metres 20
0 yards 20

Fountain of Ahmet III (Ahmet III Çeşmesi)

MAP P.26, POCKET MAP J11
Bab-ı Hümayün Cad ⊕ 1 Sultanahmet.

Situated just in front of the Bab-ı Hümayün gateway leading to the outer court of the Topkapı Palace (see page 43), this splendidly ornate, eighteenth-century Turkish Rococo fountain is the most attractive in the city. The building is almost square, with stylized, massively overhanging eaves topped by five small domes. At each corner are counters covered by ornate, curved marble window grilles, from which refreshments such as iced water and sherbets would have been handed to passers-by in the Ottoman period. These water dispensers, known as *sebil* in Turkish, were found throughout the city and often, as here, also had wall-mounted taps (*çeşme*) to provide that most basic of necessities to a local populace whose homes lacked running water.

Carpet Museum (Hali Müzesi)

MAP P.26, POCKET MAP H11
Bab-ı Hümayün Cad ⊕ 1 Sultanahmet

⊕ 0212 518 1330. Tues–Sun 9am–4pm; ₺10.

Located in the domed soup kitchens attached to the Haghia Sophia (Aya Sofya), the Carpet Museum, opened in 2013, displays a fantastic range of fine carpets and kilims woven between the fourteenth and twentieth centuries. The exhibits, many of them taken from mosques across Anatolian Turkey, are well labelled, and there is plenty of information both on how the rugs were made and the significance of the patterns with which they are decorated.

Ayasofya Hürrem (Sultan Hamami)

MAP P.26, POCKET MAP H12
Bab-ı Hümayün Cad 1 ⊕ 1 Sultanahmet
⊕ 0212 517 3535, ⓦ ayasofyahamami.com.
Daily 8am–10pm. Bath packages from €55.

Built by Sinan in 1556 for Sultan Süleyman the Magnificent, appropriately enough on the site of the Roman Baths of Zeuxippus, this beautiful hamam (**Turkish baths**) was originally intended for the faithful attending the Aya Sofya Camii. It was named after Süleyman's wife, known to Turks

Fountain of Ahmet III

as Haseki Hürrem, though better known in the west as Roxelana. In 2011, following many years of restoration, it became a working hamam once again. The building comprises two separate baths, for men and women, with entry from either end into the large, domed *camekan* or reception/changing area. Beyond this lies the main bath chamber, the *hararet*, where bathers sluice themselves down with water from a basin or "steam" on the hot *göbek taşı* ("navel stone").

Mosaic Museum Büyük (Saray Mozaikleri Müzesi)

MAP P.26, POCKET MAP H12
Torun Sok 103 ❷ 1 Sultanahmet ❷ 0212 518 1205. Tues–Sun: mid-April–Oct Tues–Sun 9am–7pm, last entry 6.30pm; Nov–mid-April 9am–5pm, last entry 4.30pm. ₺15.

The mosaics exhibited on the floor in this museum are actually *in situ*, and once formed part of a huge panel adorning the courtyard of one of the royal residences within the Great Palace complex of the Byzantine period, which sprawled all the way down the hill to the Sea of Marmara. Sections have been taken up and wall-mounted to make viewing easier, and some are so finely executed they contain 40,000 *tesserae* (mosaic pieces) per square metre. They depict quite charming scenes from everyday **Byzantine life**. In one, a stubborn goat resists the efforts of a shepherd to drag it along by its tether, in another an equally stubborn donkey turns its head away from a basket of food. Less cute are the hunting dogs bringing down a bloodied hare, leopards feasting on the carcass of an antelope and a lion tangling messily with an elephant. Although most of the mosaics here probably date from the firmly Christian sixth century, some of the scenes are pagan, Classical-era in nature, including the mythological hero Bellerophon

Mosaic in Great Palace Mosaic Museum

taking on the monstrous fire-breathing Chimera.

Arasta Bazaar

MAP P.26, POCKET MAP H12
Arasta Çarşısı 143 ❶ 1 Sultanahmet ❶ 0212 520 4046.

Originally, this long bazaar of small shops was part of the early seventeenth-century Blue Mosque complex and the revenues from it helped pay for upkeep of the mosque. An attractive market area, it's far less hassle to browse here than in the much larger Grand Bazaar. Today, there are 77 shops, selling everything from traditional Turkish carpets and kilims through to İznik tiles and Meerschaum pipes.

Church of St Sergius and Bacchus (Küçük Aya Sofya Camii)

MAP P.26, POCKET MAP G9
Küçük Aya Sofya Cad ❶ 1 Sultanahmet.
The "small mosque of Aya Sofya", as it is known in Turkish, is presumably so called because of its resemblance, on a miniature scale, to the Aya Sofya itself. It is located down the hill from the

Blue Mosque and Arasta Bazaar, close to the Sea of Marmara, and was originally the church for the nearby **Palace of Hormisdas**, a part of the Great Palace complex. Commissioned by Justinian and his consort Theodora, the church slightly predated that of Haghia Sophia, having been begun in 527 and completed in 536. The ground plan of the church is an irregular octagon, with beautiful marble columns supporting an encircling gallery, itself topped by a shallow dome oddly corrugated with alternate convex and concave ribs. Some of the capitals helping transfer the weight of the roof onto the columns are deeply incised with stylized plant motifs and the monogram of Justinian and Theodora can still be seen on a few. As it was converted into a **mosque** in the sixteenth century, nothing remains of its original mosaics, though a frieze inscribed with Greek letters honours Justinian, Theodora and St Sergius (the latter one of the two **Christian martyrs**, both soldiers who later became patron saints of the Roman army, after whom the church

Antique door, Küçük Aya Sofya Camii

was named). The proportions of the brick-built church have been spoiled by the addition, after its conversion to a mosque, of a five-domed "last prayer place" porch. Opposite the main door is a pleasant courtyard *medrese* with a teahouse.

Sokollu Mehmet Paşa Camii

MAP P.26, POCKET MAP G8
Mehmet Paşa Yokusu 🚋 1 Sultanahmet.
Tricky to find in the narrow lanes a short walk uphill from the Church of St Sergius and Bacchus, this small mosque, designed by the brilliant **Sinan** and finished in 1571, is exquisite. The courtyard, very large in proportion to the prayer hall, has at its centre a pretty ablutions fountain. It is ringed on three sides by dome-topped colonnades, beneath which are ranged the cells of a still-active boys' Koran school. The intimate prayer hall is almost square and covered by a high dome supported by four semi-domes. This interior is a model of restraint, with the finest-period İznik tiles used, sparingly, to enliven the pale stonework. Soft light filters in through the coloured glass in the tracery-work windows, and worked into the lintel above the door and embedded in the *mimber* are pieces of stone said to be from the sacred Kaaba in **Mecca**. The mosque was built for Süleyman the Magnificent's last grand vizier, Sokollu Mehmet Paşa.

Museum of Turkish and İslamic Arts (Türk Ve İslam Eserleri Müzesi)

MAP P.26, POCKET MAP G12
Atmeydanı Sok 6 🚋 1 Sultanahmet 🕿 0212 518 1805. Tues–Sun: April 9am–5pm. ₺15.
Located a little west of the Blue Mosque and flanking the Hippodrome, this impressive museum houses exhibits from the Islamic world including oriental **carpets**, illuminated

Sokullu Mehmet Paşa Camii

Korans, calligraphy, Ottoman and Persian miniatures, tiles, ceramics, metalwork, intricately carved wooden doors and mother of pearl inlaid furniture as well as ethnographical artefacts. The building is a former palace, originally home to İbrahim Paşa, grand vizier to the greatest Ottoman sultan, Süleyman the Magnificent. Completed in 1524, it was rebuilt following a devastating fire in 1843. İbrahim was the empire's most successful grand vizier and during his thirteen years in office he amassed enormous wealth. Eventually incurring the mistrust of Süleyman, the unfortunate statesman was strangled in the Topkapı Palace. Today, the museum is home to over **40,000 exhibits** dating from the earliest years of Islam in the late seventh century to today, though the main focus is on the Selçuk Turkish (eleventh to thirteenth centuries) and Ottoman (fourteenth to nineteenth centuries) periods. The major exhibition room, once the Great Hall of the palace, houses stunning Turkish carpets ranging from threadbare thirteenth-century rugs to superbly preserved giants weighing thousands of kilograms that once graced the Topkapı Palace. In the basement, the fascinating ethnography section is home to a **black goat-hair tent** woven by the nomadic *Yörük* tribes of the Taurus Mountains, descendants of the Turkoman nomads who poured into Anatolia from the eleventh century onwards.

Hippodrome at Meydanı

MAP P.26, POCKET MAP G11–12
🚊 1 Sultanahmet.

Set between the landmark Blue Mosque and the Museum of Turkish and Islamic Art, this paved, rectangular public park area was, in the Roman and Byzantine periods, a **stadium**. The original incarnation dates to 203 AD, when Emperor Septimius Severus rebuilt the city, but it was enlarged when Constantine made it the imperial capital in 330. Used during the Byzantine period for court ceremonies and games – most notably chariot racing – it was some 480m long and 117.5m wide and held up to 100,000 spectators. Spectacles in the Hippodrome were presided over by the emperor and

Egyptian obelisk at the Hippodrome at Meydani

his entourage from the *kathisma* or royal box, situated in the vicinity of what today forms the grounds of the Blue Mosque. At the northeast end of the Hippodrome, close to the tramway on Divan Yolu, is the attractive domed **Fountain of Kaiser Wilhelm II**, gifted to the then Ottoman sultan by the German leader in 1898 and located where the starting gates for the chariot races used to be. Southwest of this, following what was the central line or *spina* of the course, is the **Egyptian Obelisk**. Shipped here from Egypt in the fourth century, it is covered in hieroglyphic symbols and dates back to the sixteenth century BC. Intriguingly, it is mounted on a sandstone block carved on all four sides with images of Theodosius I, the emperor responsible for its erection, overseeing the chariot races from the royal box.

Continuing down the *spina* you'll find the **Serpentine Column**, comprising three intertwined bronze snakes, today sadly headless, though one is displayed in the city's Archeology Museum. Cast to celebrate a Greek victory over the invading Persians in 479 BC, it was brought here from Delphi by Constantine I. The last monument is a crude stone obelisk, the **Column of Constantine**, which also served as a race marker. Beyond this was a raised semicircular seating area lining the curved end of the course where the chariots turned. Known as the **sphendrome**, the seating has been subsumed by more modern buildings, but its massive substructure is visible from Nakilbent Sokak below. The course of the Hippodrome was used for state ceremonies in Ottoman times, hence its Turkish name **At Meydanı** or "square of the horses".

Blue Mosque (Sultanahmet Camii)

MAP P.26, POCKET MAP G12
Sultanahmet Meydanı ⓣ 1 Sultanahmet, ⓦ www.sultanahmetcamii.org. Closed to non-Muslims at prayer times and Friday mornings to noon. Visiting hours: 8.30–11.30am, 1–2.30pm, 3.30–4.45pm, Fridays opens at 1.30pm.

Properly known as the Sultanahmet Camii in Turkish, after the Ottoman sultan Ahmet I who commissioned it, this is probably the single most visited sight in Istanbul. Completed in 1616 after seven years' labour, the mosque takes its more tourist-friendly name from the carapace of predominantly **blue İznik tiles** liberally adorning its interior. Along with the Haghia Sophia it dominates the skyline of Sultanahmet, its majestic flow of domes and half-domes encompassed by six slender, cylindrical minarets (the latter reviled by the pious at the time of construction for consciously imitating the Great Mosque in Mecca) quite breathtaking to behold – especially when atmospherically illuminated at night. The best approach is from the Hippodrome, where a splendid doorway leads into the *avlu* or courtyard, which covers virtually the same ground area as the prayer hall itself. Only Muslims can enter the prayer hall via the main, northwest-facing door; other visitors must exit the courtyard and enter via the southwest portal, where there are often long queues. Even though non-Muslims are kept back from much of the

prayer hall by a rope barrier, the cavernous interior, with its large **central dome**, 23.5m in diameter and 43m high, flanked by four smaller semi-domes and supported by four enormous ribbed columns, is impressive. The twenty thousand-plus İznik tiles vie with each other for the visitors' attention and the prayer wall at the southeast end is pierced by the standard Mecca-facing prayer niche, the *mihrab*. To the right is the *mimber* or pulpit, used by the imam to lead prayers. To the left the loge, a raised platform for the sultan and his entourage, is connected to a royal pavilion attached to the easternmost corner of the building. Only visible from outside, this contains a suite of rooms used by the sultan on days he visited, and was reached by a sloping ramp, allowing access by horse. **Sultan Ahmet I's tomb** (Tues–Sat 9am–4pm; free), an attractively domed structure, stands in the northern corner of the grounds, accessible from Mimar Mehmet Ağa Caddesi. The sultan was buried here with his wife and three of his sons.

Cistern of the 1001 Columns

Cistern of 1001 Columns

MAP P.26, POCKET MAP G11
İmran Öktem Cad ⓘ 1 Sultanahmet ☎ 0212 518 1001. ₺20.

Despite the fact that it has been turned into a posh function space used for business meetings, gala events and weddings among other things, it's well worth having a look inside this covered cistern, another of the ones that were so crucial to the growth of Byzantine Constantinople. At around 64m by 56m, it's not quite as large as the much better known Basilica Cistern, not far to the east along Divan Yolu, but it is still the second largest in the city. The pretty, herring-bone-patterned brick domes of the vault are supported by 224 columns erected in 16 rows of 14. The total height of the interior is nearly 15m, though it is difficult to get a true impression of this as the false wooden floor, inserted when it was converted into a function space, is raised well above the original ground level. Opening hours are generally 9am–8pm daily but it is closed when there's a function taking place.

Divan Yolu

ⓘ 1 Sultanahmet.

Just north of the Cistern of 1001 Columns is Divan Yolu, today Sultanahmet's busiest thoroughfare as, despite being semi-pedestrianized (watch out for speeding service vehicles), it carries the incredibly useful T1 tramline. In Roman and Byzantine times it was the most important street in the city. Then known as the Mese or Middleway, it could be followed from the Milion (see page 24) west out of the city and on to the Adriatic. It became Divan Yolu in the Ottoman period as it led visitors and petitioners to the Divan (council) chamber in the Topkapı Palace.

On the south side of Divan Yolu is the **Firuz Ağa Camii**, one of the city's earliest mosques. Built in 1491, compared to the nearby Blue Mosque it is a model of architectural restraint, being little more than a square prayer hall surmounted by a dome attended by a single minaret. It is well used by the local faithful, and like all mosques in the city has (useful for visitors) public toilets attached.

Firuz Ağa Camii, Divan Yolu

Shops

Chez Galip

MAP P.26, POCKET MAP G12

At Meydanı 78 ⊕ 1 Sultanahmet ☎ 384 511 4577, ⓦ www.chezgalip.com. Daily 9.30am–6pm.

Sells pottery crafted in the central Anatolian pottery town of Avanos, the most intriguing of which are those based on ancient Hittite designs. There is plenty of decent-quality İznik pottery on show as well.

Cocoon

MAP P.26, POCKET MAP G9

Küçük Aya Sofya Cad 13 ⊕ 1 Sultanahmet ☎ 0212 638 6450. Daily 8am–9pm.

A positive cornucopia of richly hued artefacts made from felt – bags, hats, figurines and the like, plus an array of carpets, kilims and throws from Central Asia.

Galeri Kayseri

MAP P.26, POCKET MAP G11

Divan Yolu 58 ⊕ 1 Sultanahmet ☎ 0212 516 3366, ⓦ www.galerikayseri.com. Daily 9am–8.30pm.

The best bookshop in the old city, this is the place to come if you want a specialist book on the city – though prices are considerably higher than at home. There's another branch diagonally opposite, and both stock English-language novels.

İznik Classics

MAP P.26, POCKET MAP H12

Arasta Çarşısı ⊕ 1 Sultanahmet, ⓦ www. iznikclassics.com. Daily 9am–7pm.

İznik ceramics were, at their best, among the finest wares produced in the Ottoman Empire. The gorgeous tiles sold here today are handcrafted in the same traditional way by studio potters – and are very expensive as a result.

Jennifer's Hamam

MAP P.26, POCKET MAP H12

Arasta Çarşısı ⊕ 1 Sultanahmet ☎ 0212

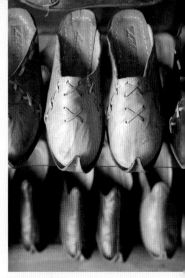

Babouches, Coccon

516 3022, ⓦ www.jennifershamam.com. Daily 9am–8pm.

Run by a friendly Canadian, the big draw here is that all the textiles are hand-woven from organic cotton, linen or silk. Choose from a bewildering range of all-cotton *peştemals*, Turkish bath wraps very popular as lightweight beach towels, traditional fluffy towels and scarves.

Yörük Collection

MAP P.26, POCKET MAP G10

Yerebatan Cad 35 ⊕ 1 Sultanahmet ☎ 0212 528 0099, ⓦ www.yoruk.com. Daily 9am–8pm.

A well-laid-out shop that tries, and mostly succeeds, in being all things to all people, with all manner of traditional (and modern interpretations of) Turkish handicrafts, from carpets to silver jewellery and Ottoman miniatures to cushion covers.

Cafés

Çiğdem Patisserie

MAP P.26, POCKET MAP G11

Divan Yolu Cad 62 ⊕ 1 Sultanahmet

☎ 0212 526 8859, ⓦ cigdempastanesi.com. Daily 9am–11pm.

This busy, continental-style patisserie is as popular with locals as visitors. Temptingly arrayed in the window are savoury snacks such as *poğaça*, soft bread rolls stuffed with cheese or a slightly spiced potato mixture; semi-sweet *tahinli ekmek*, a bread spiral coated in sweetened sesame paste; and a huge range of sweets ranging from nut-stuffed *baklava* to *acıbadem*, Turkey's monster-sized answer to Italy's Amaretto biscuit. Black tea is served good and hot in tulip-shaped glasses, and there's a decent range of coffees, from Turkish-style to a very palatable latte.

Edebiyat Kiraathanesi

MAP P.26, POCKET MAP G11
Divan Yolu Cad 14 ⓣ 1 Sultanahmet
☎ 0212514 9068. Daily 9am–10pm.

Elegant period tearooms right next to the Sultanahmet tram stop, with a superb range of Turkish desserts, coffees from Turkish (₺5) to latte (₺8), and glasses of tea (₺2). It's run by the Turkish Society for Literature, so expect cultured Turks at the next table.

Çiğdem Patisserie

Tarihi Sultanahmet Köftecisi

MAP P.26, POCKET MAP G11
Divan Yolu Cad 4 ⓣ 1 Sultanahmet ☎ 0212 511 3960. Daily 11am–11pm.

If you don't like grilled meatballs don't even consider this place. If you do, it is an Istanbul institution and one of the few places in tourist-orientated Sultanahmet to attract large numbers of Turkish diners. The owners are proud of the myriad Turkish celebrities who have eaten here, their photos and letters of thanks adorning the walls. What you get is firm *köfte* (meatballs) accompanied by a white bean salad, spicy tomato sauce, pickled peppers and crusty bread (₺17) – best chased down with the salty yoghurt drink *ayran*. Unlicensed.

The Pudding Shop

MAP P.26, POCKET MAP G11
Divan Yolu Cad 6 ⓣ 1 Sultanahmet ☎ 0212 522 2970, ⓦ www.puddingshop.com. Daily 7am–11pm.

The service is canteen-style, the queues can be long and the food OK rather than exceptional, but this bustling café played a signature role in the

hippy era as "the" hangout for travellers heading to India. The same owners still run it today, and continue serving the *sütlaç* (rice pudding) from which its unofficial name derives (it's more properly the *Lale Restaurant*). It also does a wide range of traditional savoury dishes, with mains such as *köfte* (meatballs), kebabs and stews from ₺15 – and is licensed.

Restaurants

Albura Kathisma

MAP P.26, POCKET MAP H12
Akbıyık Cad 26 ⊕ 1 Sultanahmet ⊕ 0212 517 9031, ⓦ www.alburakathisma.com. Daily 10am–11pm.

One of the best options on this bustling hotel-, restaurant- and bar-lined street, with an attractive bare-brick interior and tables outside. Service is good by Turkish standards and the wine (go for a recognized brand like Angora) reasonably priced. *Meze* include *mücver*, courgette fritters, served here in garlicky yoghurt. Traditional Anatolian dishes are the real pull, though, usually lamb or chicken based – try the lamb casserole with figs and almonds. Mains around ₺35. Licensed.

Amedros

MAP P.26, POCKET MAP G11
Hoca Rüstem Paşa Sok 7 ⊕ 1 Sultanahmet ⊕ 0212 522 8356, ⓦ www.amedroscafe.com. Daily 11am–1am.

Tucked-away up a pedestrian alleyway off Divan Yolu, this professionally run place successfully combines local and international cuisine. The subtly lit interior is effortlessly stylish, all bare-boards and neutral walls, though in summer the most popular tables are those out in the alleyway. The mixed-*meze* plate is very popular, with seven types of Turkish starters. Mains (₺30 and up) include traditional dishes such as Ottoman

chicken, served in a sweet-sour sauce with rice. Licensed. Reservations advised.

Balıkçı Sabahattin

MAP P.26, POCKET MAP H12
Seyit Hasan Kuyu Sok 1 ⊕ 1 Sultanahmet or ⊕ 1 Cankurtaran ⊕ 0212 458 1824. Daily noon–2am.

Unpromisingly located – or set in a charmingly dilapidated area of town down by the defunct railway line – whatever your view it can't be denied that this is the only Sultanahmet-area restaurant to draw monied locals from elsewhere in the city. The attraction here is freshly caught and cooked fish – from bluefish to sea bass, swordfish to red mullet – enjoyed in winter in an atmospheric old wooden house or, in summer, on tables set out front on a vine-shaded cobbled area. It's expensive, with mains ₺40 and up, but you are paying to eat alongside Istanbul's elite. Licensed. Reservations advised.

Doy Doy

MAP P.26, POCKET MAP G12
Sifa Hama Sok 13 ⊕ 1 Sultanahmet ⊕ 0212 517 1588. Daily 9am–10pm.

This four-storey restaurant serves local workers and the more impecunious visitor, concentrating on hearty portions of Turkish standards. There's *pide* (Turkish pizza, big ovals of semi-leavened *pide* bread topped with cheese or meat), plenty of kebabs, classic soups such as *mercimek çorbası* (lentil soup) and, definitely best at lunchtime, *sulu yemek* (various stews served-up from steamtrays). Mains from ₺15. Unlicensed.

Dubb

MAP P.26, POCKET MAP H11
Incili Çavuş Sok ⊕ 1 Sultanahmet ⊕ 0212513 7308, ⓦ www.dubbindian.com. Daily noon–midnight.

Indian restaurants are as rare as hens' teeth in Istanbul, so to find one so good in Sultanahmet is quite something. There are a few

Balıkçı Sabahattin

tables set out on the quiet street, otherwise dining is in a series of small rooms spread over four floors or, with fantastic views, a roof terrace. Tandoori dishes are the speciality, though there are thalis and fish dishes. Licensed. Reservations advised.

Giritli

MAP P.26, POCKET MAP H9
Kerestici Hakkı Sok ⓣ 1 Sultanahmet or ⓣ 1 Cankurtaran ⓣ 0212 458 2270. Daily noon–midnight.

The main reason to come here, and it's a worthy one, is to enjoy a full-blown set menu for ₺145 which includes all (local) alcoholic drinks, over twenty mini-*meze*, three hot starters, a grilled fish main and fruit to follow. The food, based on traditional Cretan recipes, is very good quality and the dining room is in a period wooden house, with a shady garden just across the street for alfresco summer eating. This is a good place to try *rakı*, the traditional aniseed spirit, a wonderful accompaniment to fish. Reservations advised.

Matbah

MAP P.26, POCKET MAP H11
Caferiye Sok 6/1 ⓣ 1 Sultanahmet ⓣ 0212 514 6151, ⓦ www.matbahrestaurant.com. Daily 11.30am–10.30pm.

This concept restaurant, attached to the *Ottoman Imperial Hotel*, bases all its dishes on those once prepared in the kitchens of the Topkapı Palace. Ottoman cuisine, much richer than standard contemporary Turkish cooking, used fruit in many recipes. Try *kavun dolması*, melon stuffed with lamb and pilaf rice, or *mahmudiye*, tender cinnamon-flavoured chicken served with almonds and apricots. White-clothed tables are laid out on a plant-decked terrace overlooking the leaded domes of the Cafer Ağa Theological School. Mains around ₺50. Licensed. Reservations advised.

Şirvan Sofrasi

MAP P.26, POCKET MAP G9
Küçük Ayasofya Cad 71 ⓣ 1 Sultanahmet ⓣ 0212 517 5181, ⓦ www.sirvan-sofrasit. com. Daily 10am–1am.

This restaurant has a simple and friendly ambiance and offers tasty local food. With typical Ottoman cuisine available at reasonable prices, you can try a kebab made with various meats, and opt for grilled sea bass at ₺34 and other fresh fish dishes. There are also traditional pancakes, *gozleme*, for around ₺15 to 19. The restaurant uses both stone and wooden stoves too. The food is well presented and keeps attracting both locals and tourists passing by. If you want to enjoy some water pipe, *nargile*, you can do that on the terrace.

Bars

Cozy Pub

MAP P.26, POCKET MAP G11
Divan Yolu Cad 66 ⓣ 1 Sultanahmet ⓣ 0212 520 0990, ⓦ facebook.com/ cozypubrestaurant. Daily 9am–1am.

Probably the most atmospheric bar in Sultanahmet, with a pub-like dark wood interior and plenty of tables in the narrow alley disgorging onto Divan Yolu. The beers are a tad more expensive than usual but worth it for the ambience. It also does quite reasonable international/Turkish food, including usual suspects like pasta, burgers and salads.

Istanbul Terrace Bar

MAP P.26, POCKET MAP G11
Dr Imran Oktem Cad 1 🚇 1 Sultanahmet 🚇 0212 516 9696. Daily 10am–midnight.
Opened in 2013 after a long period of restoration, the terrace bar of the Arcadia Blue Hotel gives one of the best vantage points in the city. To the southeast the Sea of Marmara glimmers behind the Hippodrome and Blue Mosque, straight ahead the Haghia Sophia and grounds of the Topkapı Palace are backed by distant Asia, and to the northeast stretches the thin ribbon of the Bosphorus. It all looks particularly appealing, conveniently enough for those in need of a drink at the end of a day's exploration, as the sun goes down.

Just Bar

MAP P.26, POCKET MAP H12
Akbıyık Cad 28 🚇 0532 387 5729. Daily 10am–2pm.
This lively bar is very popular with guests from the myriad hotels and hostels in this popular neighbourhood. There's a small seating area fronting the busy street, perfect for people-watching on warm evenings, and inside the tables are cleared to make a small dancefloor on weekend nights. Beers ₺14.

Pierre Loti Roof-Bar

MAP P.26, POCKET MAP G8
Piyer Loti Cad 5 🚇 1 Sultanahmet 🚇 0212 518 5700. Daily 11am–midnight.
Hotel bars seldom drip character and this place, though smart, is no exception. But the vistas over Istanbul's exotic skyline are fabulous – best enjoyed at sunset. It's quite pricey, but your drink comes accompanied by a bowl of quality *çerez* (salted Turkish nibbles that usually include roasted chickpeas, peanuts, almonds and pistachios).

SULTANAHMET

Pierre Loti Roof-Bar

Topkapı Palace to the Golden Horn

Superbly located on the first of the old city's seven hills, right at the snout of the peninsula pointing up the continent-dividing Bosphorus strait, the Topkapı Palace was the nerve centre of the powerful Ottoman Empire. This sprawling, walled compound encompasses not only the courtyards and pavilions of the palace itself but also Istanbul's excellent Archeology Museum, an important Byzantine church and Gülhane Park, the only major green and open space in the congested old city. Following the busy tramline downhill to the northwest, you come to the more workaday business district of Sirkeci, best known to visitors for its late nineteenth-century station, once the easternmost terminus of the famous Orient Express. Beyond it, fronting the ferry-filled waters of the Golden Horn, is mega-bustling Eminönü, with its fragrant, Ottoman-era Spice Bazaar.

Archeology Museum (Arkeoloji Müzesi)

MAP P.44, POCKET MAP H7
Osman Hamdi Bey Yokuşu ☉ 1 Gülhane ☎ 0212 520 7740, ⓦ istanbularkeoloji.gov. tr. Tues–Sun: April–Oct 9am–7pm; Nov–March 9am–5pm. t20, audio-guides t10.

Reached either from the first court of the Topkapı Palace or via the main entrance to Gülhane Park, this fascinating but often overlooked museum comprises three separate sections, each housed in a historic building. The first, on your left as you enter, is the small **Museum of the Ancient Orient**, built in 1883. Pick of the exhibits is a clay tablet inscribed in cuneiform, copied from a silver original, marking a treaty signed between the Hittites and Egyptians after a major battle in 1269 BC. This was the world's first known peace treaty, and a copy is housed in the UN headquarters in New York. The blue and yellow glazed bricks, decorated with animals in raised relief and dating to the reign of Nebuchadnezzar (604–562 BC), once formed a frieze lining the processional way to Babylon's Ishtar Gate. The monumental Neoclassical-style building on the right as you head into the grounds was built by French architect Vallaury in 1891. This is the main building of the **Archeology Museum** complex, and contains a stunning array of artefacts ranging from the Paleolithic to the Ottoman periods. Unmissable, on the ground floor, are the **Sidon Sarcophagi**, discovered in what is today Lebanon in the late nineteenth century. The relief-carving on the surfaces of the Alexander, Lycian and Mourning Women sarcophagi is quite superb. Also on the ground floor is a comprehensive display of marble statuary from the Archaic to Roman periods. Upstairs the excellent **Istanbul through the Ages** exhibition is a compulsory introduction to the city's complex history, and includes oddities like a bronze snake-head from the Serpentine Column in the Hippodrome (see page 33) and a section of the chain stretched across the Golden Horn in Byzantine times to prevent enemy shipping entering. Also worth seeking out are the **Byzantine collection** in the semi-basement and the **Anatolia and Troy through the Ages** exhibition on the second floor. Opposite the main building is the third museum in the complex, the **Museum of Turkish Ceramics**. Built in the fifteenth century as part of the Topkapı Palace complex and known as the Çinili Köşk or Tiled Pavilion, it houses a vibrant display of Turkish tiles and other ceramic wares.

Haghia Eirene (Aya İrini)

MAP P.44, POCKET MAP H7
Mon & Wed–Sun: April–Oct 9am–7pm; Nov–March 9am–4.30pm. ₺20.
The predominantly brick-built Haghia Eirene or "Church of the Holy Peace", is tucked away in the northwest corner of the first court of the Topkapı Palace. One of the earliest churches in Constantinople, it burned down in the same 532 riot that destroyed the second incarnation of the Haghia Sophia (see page 25) and was rebuilt in its current form soon after. It is rectangular in shape and topped by a relatively small dome surmounted on a drum. Inside, the most prominent features are the simple black on gold mosaic cross in the apse and, below it, a curved seating area for the clergy, the synthronon.

Topkapı Palace (Topkapı Sarayı)

MAP P.44, POCKET MAP J7
Topkapı Sarayı Müzesi ⊕ 1 Sultanahmet ⊕ 0212 512 0480, ⓦ topkapisarayi.gov. tr. Daily except Tues: mid-April–Oct 9am–6.45pm; Nov–mid-April 9am–4.45pm. ₺60, audio-guides ₺20.
Completed in 1465, this palace complex, a collection of buildings ranged around four large courtyards, was the administrative

Haghia Eirene

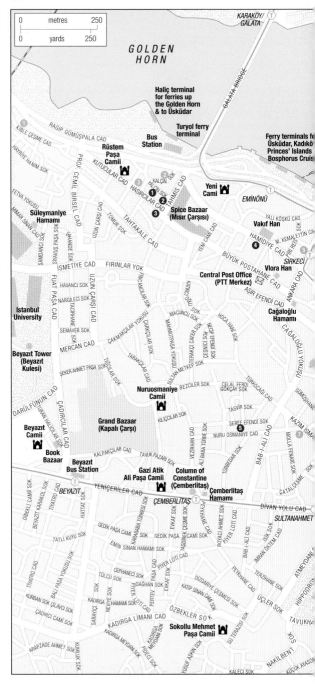

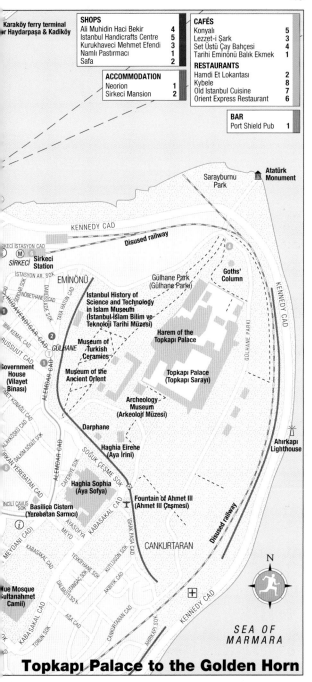

SHOPS	
Ali Muhidin Haci Bekir	4
Istanbul Handicrafts Centre	5
Kurukhaveci Mehmet Efendi	3
Namlı Pastırmacı	1
Safa	2

ACCOMMODATION	
Neorion	1
Sirkeci Mansion	2

CAFÉS	
Konyalı	5
Lezzet-i Şark	3
Set Üstü Çay Bahçesi	4
Tarihi Eminönü Balık Ekmek	1

RESTAURANTS	
Hamdi Et Lokantası	2
Kybele	8
Old Istanbul Cuisine	7
Orient Express Restaurant	6

BAR	
Port Shield Pub	1

Topkapı Palace to the Golden Horn

Karaköy ferry terminal or Haydarpaşa & Kadiköy

Sarayburnu Park — Atatürk Monument

KENNEDY CAD

Disused railway

SİRKECİ — Sirkeci Station — İSTASYON AR. SOK

EMİNÖNÜ

Gülhane Park (Gülhane Parkı) — Goths' Column

İstanbul History of Science and Technology in Islam Museum (İstanbul İslam Bilim ve Teknoloji Tarihi Müzesi)

Harem of the Topkapı Palace

GÜLHANE — Museum of Turkish Ceramics

Museum of the Ancient Orient

Topkapı Palace (Topkapı Sarayı)

Government House (Vilayet Binası)

Archeology Museum (Arkeoloji Müzesi)

Darphane

Haghia Eirene (Aya İrini)

SOĞUK ÇEŞME SOK

Ahırkapı Lighthouse

Haghia Sophia (Aya Sofya)

Fountain of Ahmet III (Ahmet III Çeşmesi)

Basilica Cistern (Yerebatan Sarnıcı)

CANKURTARAN

Blue Mosque (Sultanahmet Camii)

Disused railway

KENNEDY CAD

SEA OF MARMARA

N

Topkapı Palace

1 Ortakapı or Middle Gate
2 Kitchens and Cooks' Quarters
3 Stables and Harness Rooms
4 Barrack of the Halberdiers of the Long Tresses
5 Hall of the Divan
6 Offices of the Divan
7 Inner Treasury
8 Gate of Felicity (Bâb-üs Saadet)
9 Throne Room
10 Library of Sultanahmet III
11 Rooms of the Relics of the Prophet
12 Imperial Treasury (Pavilion of Mehmet II)
13 Hall of the Expeditionary Force
14 Circumcision Köşkü
15 Baghdad Köşkü
16 Revan Köşkü
17 Tulip Gardens of Ahmet III
18 Mustafa Paşa Köşkü
19 Mecidiye Köşkü
20 Entry to the Harem (Carriage Gate)
21 Aviary Gate (Kushane Kapisi)
22 Valide Sultan's Court
23 Valide Sultan's Dining Room
24 Valide Sultan's Bedroom
25 Golden Road
26 Ahmet III Dining Room

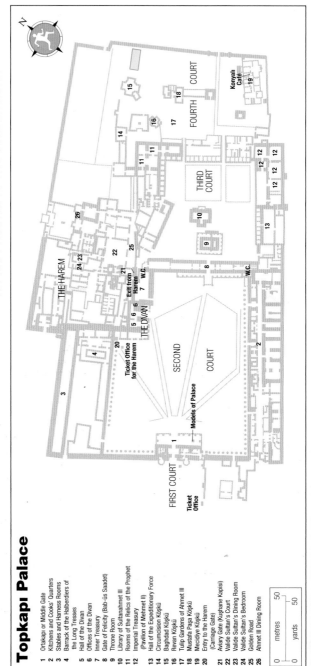

and political heart of the Ottoman Empire until 1853, when the sultan decamped to the European-style Dolmabahçe Palace across the Golden Horn. Along with neighbours the Haghia Sophia and Blue Mosque, it's the most visited sight in Istanbul. Enter the **first court** (free admission) by the Bab-ı-Hümayün, a gateway piercing the defensive wall which separated the palace from the city. This area was home to the bakeries and imperial mint. The ticket office for the remainder of the courts is in the wall to the right of the Bab-ı Selam or **Gate of Salutations**, with its fairy-tale-like conical turrets. Inside the gate are a couple of models of the palace complex, useful for orientation. The **second court** is flanked to the right by the kitchens, to the left are the Privy Stables and the Divan. The latter, beautifully decorated in sixteenth-century Ottoman style, was the council chamber where the chief officials (viziers) met to discuss matters of state, secretly watched from a grilled window in the wall behind by the sultan.

Next door, the inner treasury is now the **Armoury Museum**. Court ceremonies were presided over, and military campaigns launched, by the sultan seated on his throne in front of the Babüs Saadet or **Gate of Felicity**. Beyond this, the **third court** was the nerve centre of the Ottoman-era palace as it contained both the Palace School, which trained the empire's officials, as well as the **Throne Room** where decisions taken in the Divan were sealed by the sultan. Behind the Throne Room is the pretty **Library of Sultanahmet III**. The **Rooms of the Relics of the Prophet** in the northwest corner of the court contain the mantle and standard of the Prophet Mohammed, among many other holy relics, while **the Imperial Treasury** to the right is now home to treasures amassed by the sultans over the centuries, including the famed Topkapı Dagger and Spoonmaker's Diamond. The **Hall of the Expeditionary Force**, in the same row as the treasury, contains some splendid costumes worn by various sultans.

TOPKAPI PALACE TO THE GOLDEN HORN

Circumcision Room (Topkapı Palace)

The fourth court was devoted to leisure, comprising a series of **pavilions** set in pretty gardens, including the Baghdad, Revan and Circumcision pavilions. A fourth, the Mecidiye, houses the expensive *Konyalı Café & Restaurant*, with its fine views across the Bosphorus to Asia.

Harem of the Topkapı Palace

MAP P.44, POCKET MAP H6
Topkapı Palace, second court ⚈ 1
Sultanahmet. Daily except Tues: mid-April–Oct 9am–6.45pm; Nov–mid-April 9am–4.45pm. ₺35.

Owing to its location within the grounds of the Topkapı Palace's second court, you can't visit the **women's quarters** or Harem (literally meaning "forbidden" in Arabic) without first paying to enter the palace itself. The Harem was a suite of rooms within the palace complex, over four hundred of them, where the sultan's wives, female slaves (concubines) and children resided. It also contained the quarters of the Black Eunuchs who guarded them, and the private quarters of the sultan. Largely

constructed during the reign of Murat III in the late sixteenth century, the Harem is thus a century or so more recent than the Topkapı Palace. The ticket office is by the distinctive Divan Tower, entry through the **Carriage Gate**, so called because this is where the concubines mounted carriages for trips out. Leading right through the maze-like complex, from its entrance in the second court to its exit in the third, is a cobbled path known as the Golden Way, purportedly named after a new sultan's habit of throwing gold coins to his concubines. The first important suite of rooms are those of the **Valide Sultan** (the sultan's mother), ranged around a spacious courtyard. North of here are the apartments and reception rooms of the sultan himself. Largest of these is the **Imperial Hall**, lush with Baroque gilt and İznik tiles, where the sultan entertained visitors. More beautiful though is **Murat III's Salon**, designed by Sinan in 1578 and boasting a stunning bronze fireplace and walls gleaming with finest-period İznik tiles. The small, domed **Library of**

Gülhane Park

İznik tiles

Both the Topkapı Palace and its Harem gleam with them, as does the Rüstem Paşa Camii, the Sokollu Mehmet Paşa Camii and scores of Ottoman-era buildings across the city. The Blue Mosque even derives its "English" name from the predominantly blue İznik tiles sheathing its interior. Production began in İznik (ancient Nicea) on the south shores of the Sea of Marmara in the fifteenth century and soon these tiles, inspired by Persian designs and made mostly from quartz rather than clay, became all the rage. So much so that by the sixteenth century there were over three hundred kilns churning out top-quality tiles (and other ceramics), often decorated with blue stylized flowers or geometric shapes on a white ground, enlivened by splashes of vivid red. Quality and output peaked in the late sixteenth and early seventeenth centuries. After a long period of decline, studio-potters based in İznik have revived the art.

Ahmet I (1608–09) is exquisite, as is the **dining room of Ahmet III**, probably so called because of the bowls of fruit painted on the wood-panelled walls. The notorious Cage, where the sultan's brothers were confined to avoid squabbles between potential successors to the throne, was probably located in rooms on the first floor, closed to visitors. Exit the complex through the **Aviary Gate**.

Gülhane Park (Gülhane Parki)

MAP P.44, POCKET MAP H6
Alemdar Cad ⊙ 1 Gülhane.

Once the extended gardens of the Topkapı Palace, today Gülhane Park makes a great place to escape the tourist bustle of the big-hitter sights on the crown of the hill above. A few pieces of distinctly average play equipment for young kids aside, there's little to do except unwind, though it's worth strolling down to the **Goths' Column** in the northeast of the park, not far from the tip of the peninsula at Saray Burnu (Palace Point). Built to commemorate a third- or fourth-century victory over said Goths, it is over 18m high and topped by a large, intricately carved Corinthian capital. Nearby is *Set Üstü Çay*

Bahçesi (see page 56), a decent tea garden with great views up the Bosphorus and across to Asia.

Istanbul History of Science and Technology in Islam Museum (İstanbul İslam Bilim ve Teknoloji Tarihi Müzesi)

MAP P.44, POCKET MAP H6
Gülhane Parkı ⊙ 1 Gülhane ⊙ 0212 528 8065. Mon & Wed–Sun: mid-April–Oct 9am–6.30pm; Nov–mid-April 9am–4.30pm. ₺12.

Showcasing the invaluable contribution made to civilization by scientists and inventors from the Islamic world between the eighth and sixteenth centuries, this museum is housed in what were the imperial stables, built into the inside of the walls encircling Gülhane Park. If you're looking for genuine artefacts, be prepared to be disappointed, as all the exhibits are meticulous models made at Johann Wolfgang von Goethe University, Frankfurt. The replicas are impressive, however, and are beautifully displayed artworks in their own right, not least an elephant-shaped water clock based on a twelfth-century original and a planetarium based on an idea by tenth-century astronomer as-Siğzi.

Cağaloğlu Hamamı

MAP P.44, POCKET MAP G6
Kazım İsmail Gürkan Cad 34 ● 1
Sultanahmet ● 0212 522 2424,
● cagalogluhamami.com.tr. Mon–Fri
9am–10pm, Sat & Sun 9am–11pm. Baths
from €30.

Some 400m north of Divan Yolu, these Turkish baths are probably the most famous in the city, not least because *Indiana Jones and the Temple of Doom* included a scene shot in this hamam, and luminaries as varied as Florence Nightingale and John Travolta are reputed to have bathed here. It was built in 1741 during the reign of Sultan Mahmut I in Ottoman Baroque style, and its profits were used to fund the sultan's library in the Aya Sofya Camii. In an era when only the very richest citizens had private baths, establishments such as these were essential for both cleanliness and hygiene and not, as they are today, merely an (admittedly thoroughly pleasurable) afterthought to a day's sightseeing. Bathers begin in the *camekan*, the largest room in the bathhouse, surmounted by a large dome, where there are changing rooms and areas to relax with tea or other refreshments. Beyond the small *soğukluk* or cold room is the main event, the *hararet* or steam room, presided over by a large dome supported by a circle of columns, which diffuses soft light through the tiny, round glass windows studding it. The bathhouse comprises two sections, with separate entrances and bathing rooms for men and women.

Alemdar Street (Alemdar Caddesi)

MAP P.44, POCKET MAP H7
● 1 Gülhane.

The lower part of this street, from where it curves around past the main entrance to Gülhane Park, has a few points of interest

up and down it when crossing. The first, actually just above the park entrance, is the **Zeynep Sultan Camii**. At first sight this attractive building looks very much like a Byzantine church, with its contrasting bands of brick and pale-coloured stone and scallop-edged dome. It is in fact a mosque, built in 1769 by Zeynep, daughter of Sultan Ahmet III. Not far below it is a small, domed and extremely pretty **marble kiosk** (*büfe* in Turkish) selling cigarettes, gum, tissues and the like. In the Ottoman period this was a *sebil*, from which free water was handed out to passers-by. These *sebil*s were dotted throughout the city, donated by wealthy citizens who hoped to secure their place in paradise through their good deeds. A short way down the street is a grand gateway on the left, notable for its sinuous, Baroque-style overhanging roof – the **Bab-ı Ali** – remodelled in 1843. From the mid-eighteenth century onwards, this gate led to the personal quarters and offices of the grand vizier, the chief official of the Ottoman Empire, where most state business was handled – an institution which became known to the West as the Sublime Porte. Opposite is the **Alay Köşk**, built into the line of walls now surrounding the park but which were originally the outer fortifications of the Topkapı Palace, built in 1465 by Mehmet the Conqueror. Beautifully restored in 2011, this polygonal structure allowed suspicious sultans to observe the comings and goings of the Sublime Porte opposite. The more trusting used it to review the great processions held in the city, such as that of the Guilds, involving virtually every tradesman in the city and held every fifty years or so. Deli İbrahim, or İbrahim the Mad (1640–48), is reputed to have shot passers-by with a crossbow from this eyrie.

Men getting massages in Cağaloğlu Hamamı

Access is from inside the park, with a sloping ramp allowing the sultan to enter without dismounting.

Sirkeci Station

MAP P.44, POCKET MAP G6
Ankara Cad ⊕ 1 Sirkeci.

The eastern terminus of the fabled Orient Express, which first terminated here in 1888 after its 2900km journey from Paris via Vienna, Sirkeci Station has withstood the vicissitudes of time remarkably well. Intact are its clock towers, Moorish arches and Parisian-style domed roof, a surprisingly successful architectural hotchpotch of Neoclassical and Islamic architecture, designed by the Prussian architect August Jachmund. Many distinguished visitors once arrived at Sirkeci Station from Europe, including King Boris III of Bulgaria and Agatha Christie, the latter immortalizing the service in *Murder on the Orient Express*. Today, the station serves neither kings nor famous authors, or indeed overground trains. But inside this iconic station building is the Sirkeci stop on the Marmaray metro line (see page 148) which connects Europe to Asia via the Bosphorus tunnel. There's also a small museum (Tues–Sun 9am–5pm; free) for rail buffs (see page 148).

Central Sirkeci

MAP P.44, POCKET MAP G6
Sirkeci Merkez ⊕ 1 Sirkeci.

The heart of this bustling commercial district, centred on two major streets, Büyük Postane Caddesi and Hamidiye Caddesi, offers some early twentieth-century delights. Built in 1909 and easiest to find is the monumental **PTT Merkez** or **Central Post Office** on Büyük Postane Caddesi. It was designed by Paris-trained Turk Vedat Tak, an exponent of the First National Architectural Movement, which sought to blend Ottoman and western styles to produce original buildings representative of the rapidly modernizing empire. With its imposing stone facade combining Ottoman elements such as İznik tiles with Neoclassical Corinthian pilasters, it certainly succeeds. The inside of the building, with its glazed roof and period fittings, is worth a look even if you're not buying stamps. Diagonally opposite the PTT Merkez is an overtly European-style import, the Art Nouveau **Vlora Han**, today a run-down office block which nonetheless still impresses with its curved facade, panels of stylized roses in raised-relief plasterwork and whiplash wrought-iron balcony rails. Far more austere is the **Vakıf Han** on Hamidiye Caddesi. Built as a seven-storey office block to a design by another principal exponent of the First National Architectural Movement,

Kemaleddin Bey, its severe stone facade, leavened by Ottoman-style domed turrets, conceals a steel skeleton.

Spice Bazaar (Mısır Çarşısı)

MAP P.44, POCKET MAP F6

Cami Meydanı ① 1 Eminönü. ① 0212 513 6597, ⓦ www.misircarsisi.org.tr. Daily 8am–7.30pm.

Close to the waterfront in Eminönü, the Spice Bazaar (*Mısır Çarşısı*) was built as part of the Yeni Cami complex, the revenues raised from it used to fund the running of the mosque and its associated philanthropic institutions. The L-shaped building is typically Ottoman in style, with 88 vaulted chambers and more rooms above, usually entered by a monumental gateway at the northeast corner. The origins of its name are uncertain. *Mısır* in

Spice Bazaar

Turkish can mean either corn or Egypt, and it's possible this name derives either from the fact that in the Byzantine period the area was the centre of corn trading or that many of the spices imported into Istanbul came from Egypt. Today, the bazaar still sells myriad spices, usually attractively piled in mounds of contrasting colours (and smells) outside the hole-in-the-wall cells within, alongside other tempting goodies like Turkish delight and pistachio nuts. Prices are high, however, as this is the most popular market in the city after the Grand Bazaar, so look as the locals do in the surrounding streets for cheaper buys.

Around the Spice Bazaar

MAP P.44, POCKET MAP F6
🚊 1 Eminönü.

Keen shoppers should peruse **Tahmis Caddesi**, a row of stalls lining the western wall of the bazaar selling a huge variety of traditional Turkish cheeses, olives, nuts and spices as well as cured meats. There's more of the same on narrow **Hasırcılar Caddesi** (Street of the Strawmakers) running northwest of the bazaar. On the corner of Tahmis and Hasırcılar streets is the ever-busy coffee emporium *Kurukhaveci Mehmet Efendi* (see page 55), in one of Istanbul's few Art Deco buildings.

On the east side of the Spice Bazaar is a fascinating market, the **garden and pet bazaar**, which sells everything from caged goldfinches to chicks dyed the colours of the city's big football teams (a yellow chick and a red one would be for Galatasaray, a yellow and a blue for Fenerbahçe). You might even spot a leech wriggling in a jar.

Yeni Cami

MAP P.44, POCKET MAP G6
Yeni Cami Cad 🚊 1 Eminönü.

The domes and minarets of the "New Mosque" soon become a familiar landmark to visitors heading up or across the Bosphorus, or trundling over the Galata Bridge to Galata/Beyoğlu on the north side of the Golden Horn, and the steps outside it are invariably busy, not least with purveyors of seed to feed the thousands of pigeons that flock into the square in front of it. This was the last of the imperial mosques to be built in the city, hence its name, and although construction began in 1597, it wasn't completed until 1663. Like its predecessors, it was part of a complex to provide for the needs of the local community, comprising a hospital, soup kitchen, baths and fountains and, of course, the Spice Bazaar. Designed by an apprentice of the Ottoman Empire's master architect Sinan, the mosque follows convention, with the faithful first entering a large courtyard centred on a ritual ablutions fountain and surrounded on three sides by porticoes. The prayer hall, fronted by a raised platform covered by a portico for late comers or when the interior is packed, is cruciform in plan, the central dome flanked by four semi-domes.

Galata Bridge

MAP P.44, POCKET MAP F5
Eminönü 🚊 1 Eminönü or Karaköy.

The entire Eminönü waterfront heaves with humanity: kindly souls feeding pigeons in the square; the faithful heading to prayers in the Yeni Cami; commuters rushing to catch a ferry home to Asia, having elbowed their way to the best buys in the packed, narrow alleys around the Spice Bazaar; vendors flogging knock-off wares in one of the underpasses; and hungry visitors munching on cut-price fish sandwiches on the quay. So it's little surprise that the **Galata Bridge**, while far from being the most elegant or historic bridge in the world, is one of its busiest and most vibrant, accommodating as it does the overspill from the congested waterfront area. The lower deck is lined with cafés and restaurants, while the upper deck teems with anglers and itinerants peddling fake Adidas socks and gimcrack watches, shouting to be heard above the roar of trucks and rumble of the tram. The first bridge, built of wood in 1845, was some 500m long and symbolically linked the Muslim-dominated old city with the Christianized European quarters of Galata and Pera (Beyoğlu). Today's steel version dates back to the 1980s, and the central section can be hoisted to allow big ships access to the Golden Horn.

Rüstem Paşa Camii

MAP P.44, POCKET MAP F5

Hasırcılar Çarşısı ⬤ 1 Eminönü.

Dating back to 1561, internally this is one of the most attractive mosques in the whole of Istanbul. Another Sinan masterpiece, it is cleverly constructed on a raised terrace above the level of the alleys below. Built for Rüstem Paşa, the grand vizier of Süleyman the Magnificent in 1561, the mosque is reached by steps leading through a passageway to the terrace, which is dominated by an unusual double portico. The entrance for visitors is through a side-door to the left of the building. Essentially a simple dome supported by four large piers, its real wonder is the finest-period İznik tiles covering virtually every available surface. As usual, predominantly blue on a white ground, many of these tiles are embellished by the addition of vivid red, slightly raised-relief details. As this colour was very tricky for the craftsman to achieve, they represent the high point of İznik tile production.

Fishermen on Galata Bridge

Shops

Ali Muhidin Haci Bekir

MAP P.44, POCKET MAP G6
Hamidiye Cad 83 ⓘ 1 Eminönü ☎ 0216
379 4921. Mon–Sat 9am–7.30pm, Sun
9am–9pm.

This is not the cheapest place to
buy traditional *lokum* (Turkish
delight) but it is one of the
best. Established way back in
1717, this charming shop stocks
twenty-plus flavours of the sticky
stuff, all colourfully displayed
in a shop interior lined with
old-fashioned wood shelves and
glass-fronted cabinets. There's
much more than *lokum* here
too, including traditional boiled
sweets, hazelnut-paste goodies and
sugared almonds.

Istanbul Handicrafts Centre

MAP P.44, POCKET MAP G7
Nuruosmaniye Cd 32 5 ⓘ 1 Sultanahmet.
Daily 9am–8pm.

Housed in a restored *medrese*
(Islamic theological school), this
centre keeps alive traditional crafts
such as bookbinding, marbling and
calligraphy. It's worth visiting to
see the building and the artisans
at work, even if you choose not to
purchase anything.

Kurukhaveci Mehmet Efendi

MAP P.44, POCKET MAP F5
Tahmis Sok 66 ⓘ 1 Eminönü ☎ 0212 511
4262, ⓦ mehmetefendi.com. Mon–Sat
9am–7pm.

An Istanbul institution, this is the
place to come if you want to buy
coffee roasted and ground the way
it should be to make both genuine
Turkish and filter coffee. The
queues of locals from across the city
attest to its quality. This Art Deco
period gem of a shop also sells
sahlep, a powdered orchid-root-
based beverage popular in Istanbul's
cold winters.

Kurukahveci Mehmet Efendi

Namlı Pastırmacı

MAP P.44, POCKET MAP F5
Hasırcılar Cad 14 ⓘ 1 Eminönü ☎ 0212 511
6393, ⓦ namlipastirma.com.tr. Mon–Sat
7.30am–8pm.

One of the best delicatessens in
the city, established in 1929, it
sells a very wide range of cheeses
from across the country (and some
imported), a cornucopia of cured
meats, including garlicky *pastırma*
(a form of pastrami) and *sucuk*
(a spicy sausage ring traditionally
sliced and cooked up with eggs),
as well as more prosaic items like
olives, olive oil and pickles.

Safa

MAP P.44, POCKET MAP F5
Hasırcılar Cad 10 ⓘ 1 Eminönü. ☎ 0212
527 2277. Daily 8am–8pm.

Not so famous as *Karaköy Güllüöğlu*
across the Golden Horn and
consequently considerably cheaper,
this is a great place to stock up
on walnut-filled *baklava* or *fıstık
sarması*, rolls of paper-thin filo
pastry wrapped around a delicious
pistachio filling. They also do
more inexpensive favourites such
as *tulumba*, a kind of corrugated
donut roll soaked in syrup.

Tarihi Eminönü Balık Ekmek

Cafés

Konyalı

MAP P.44, POCKET MAP G6
Ankara Cad 4 🚇 1 Sirkeci ☎ 0212 527
1935. Mon–Sat 6am–9pm.
Opposite the entrance to Sirkeci
Station, this traditional *pastane* has
been supplying breakfasts, lunches
and on-the-way-home snacks to
local office workers and traders
for decades. The tea comes in
tulip-shaped glasses and there's a
wide range of bread-based delights
to choose from, such as bagel-like
sesame seed-studded *simit* and
lasagne-like *su böreği* (₺9 a portion),
layers of boiled pastry filled with
goat's cheese and parsley. Attached
is the sister *Konyalı Lokantası*,
a traditional Turkish restaurant
dating back to 1897.

Lezzet-i Şark

MAP P.44, POCKET MAP F5
Hasırcılar Cad 38 🚇 1 Eminönü ☎ 0212
514 2763, 🌐 www.lezzetisark.com. Daily
7am–8.30pm
Unsophisticated but excellent
bazaar eating establishment dishing
up delicious specialities from
Gaziantep, Turkey's food capital.
Start off with bulgur wheat-
wrapped meatballs (*içli köfte*) and
finish with the sweetened cheese
and shredded wheat dessert *künefe*
– perhaps with a succulent kebab
sandwiched between. No alcohol.
Mains from ₺14.

Set Üstü Çay Bahçesi

MAP P.44, POCKET MAP J6
Gülhane Parkı 🚇 1 Gülhane ☎ 0212 513
9610. Daily 9am–10pm.
This open-air café is rarely visited
by tourists as it is hidden away in
the northeast corner of Gülhane
Park, near the Goths' Column.
This is a shame as the tea here,
brought to the table samovar-style,
is delicious and the views across
to Asia and up the Bosphorus
are lovely. It also does basic food
including *köfte* (grilled meatballs)
and toasted sandwiches (₺8).

Tarihi Eminönü Balık Ekmek

MAP P.44, POCKET MAP E5
Turyol İskele Yanı 🚇 1 Eminönü ☎ 0216
541 0352. Daily 8.30am–1am.
Set up right on the quay front just
to the left of the entrance to the

Galata Bridge, this simple café has combined tradition – it began across the Bosphorus in Asia in 1948 – with twenty-first-century business savvy, relocating to its present location in 2007 to take advantage of the huge numbers of visitors milling around the Eminönü waterfront. Enjoy a cheap fish sandwich served by staff in faux-Ottoman brocade-decorated attire.

Restaurants

Hamdi et Lokantası

MAP P.44, POCKET MAP F5
Kalçın Sok 17 🖲 1 Eminönü 🖲 0212 658 8011. Daily noon–11pm.
Set back from the Eminönü waterfront, this traditional restaurant specializing in southeast Turkish food serves up some of the best kebabs (over twenty varieties of them) and accompaniments in the central part of the old city, and has quality *baklava* for dessert. Tables on the upper floors of this five-storey establishment have good views across the Galata Bridge and Golden Horn. It's expensive by kebab-joint standards (mains ₺32 and up) and some diners have reported off-hand service. Licensed.

Kybele

MAP P.44, POCKET MAP G11
Yerebatan Cad 23 🖲 1 Sultanahmet 🖲 0212 511 7766. Daily 8am–midnight.
The uniquely eccentric ambiance of this restaurant is something unforgettable and magical. There are countless lamps in the ceiling, stacks of trinkets and intricate carpets on the floors - it feels as if you've entered some old Turkish fairytale. Upstairs there's a beautiful terrace too. Take a seat in one of the nooks and crannies of the spacious interior and enjoy a traditional meal.

Old Istanbul Cuisine

MAP P.44, POCKET MAP G10

Gürkan Cad 13 🖲 1 Sultnahmet 🖲 535 263 9846. Daily 10.10am–11.55pm.
A restaurant with a cosy, charming decor, located very conveniently near both the Blue Mosque, Haghia Sophia and Sokollu Mehmet Paşa Camii and quite close to the Topkapı Palace. The perfect place to have a rest after a long day of sightseeing. Enjoy a cup of apple tea and a bite of sweet *baklava* after a tasty meal of traditional kebab or fish.

Orient Express Restaurant

MAP P.44, POCKET MAP H6
İstasyon Cad, Sirkeci Gar 2 🖲 0212 522 2280, 🌐 www.orientexpressrestaurant.net. Daily 7.30am–midnight.
The nineteenth-century, European-designed restaurant is based inside Sirkeci Station, which was in the not too distant past the last stop for the world-famous Orient Express. It's a truly atmospheric location to tuck into a variety of traditional Turkish dishes. Kebabs start at ₺30, while *köfte* are a shade cheaper at ₺25. The Orient Express Restaurant is licensed too, with wine by the glass starting from ₺15, and beers ranging from ₺12–14.

Bar

Port Shield Pub

MAP P.44, POCKET MAP H10
Ebusuud Cad 2 🖲 1 Gülhane 🖲 0212 512 7050. Daily 10.30am–1.30am.
This perennially popular sports bar is handily located opposite the Gülhane tramstop. It's a well-run establishment that does its best to recreate the atmosphere of an English pub. Flyers advertising the upcoming sports events being shown on the big screens are plastered to the outside walls – everything from English football matches through rugby to cricket and American football. It also has a typical pub-grub menu.

Grand Bazaar District

This sprawling area of the old city contains one of Istanbul's best-known and most-visited buildings, the ever-busy Grand Bazaar, reputedly the largest covered historic bazaar in the world – and fifteenth-century forerunner of today's shopping mall. Its real jewel, however, stands in imposing grandeur on top of the third hill of the old city – the Süleymaniye, a mosque complex of near architectural perfection. Viewing the silhouette of its cascading domes and bristling minarets from across the Golden Horn at sunset is stunning, and an intimate walk around its hallowed grounds is moving. North and west of the Grand Bazaar a rather grittier area, merging into the business district of Aksaray, is embellished by some important Ottoman mosques along with a few Byzantine-era gems, which are all the more enjoyable to explore as so few visitors make the effort to get off the beaten track.

Süleymaniye Mosque Complex (Süleymaniye Külliyesi)

MAP P.60, POCKET MAP E6
Prof Siddik Sami Onar Cad, Vefa ☉ 1
Beyazıt or Laleli/Üniversite Ⓜ 2 Vezneciler
☎ 0212 514 0139.

Northwest of the Grand Bazaar, the Süleymaniye Külliyesi (mosque complex) is best reached by walking up from the Laleli/Üniversite tramstop, first along Büyük Reşit Paşa Caddesi, then onto 16 Mart Şehit and Süleymaniye Caddesi. En route you'll pass the **Kalenderhane Camii**, a distinctive brick-built mosque once the thirteenth-century Byzantine Church of Kyriotissa, and under an arch of the fourth-century Aqueduct of Valens (see page 66). At the top is **Tıryakı Çarşısı**, "market of the addicts", a street in front of the mosque named after the opium addicts who puffed away their lives here. You are now in the **Süleymaniye Mosque Complex,** a group of buildings with the

mosque at its heart, arguably the pinnacle of achievement of the architect Sinan, and worthy legacy of the sultan who founded it, Süleyman the Magnificent. Begun in 1550 on a tricky hilltop site, it took seven years to complete. Entering the **Süleymaniye Camii** by the side door, it's hard not to be impressed by the sheer sense of space the architect has achieved by cleverly hiding the piers supporting the massive dome (53m high by 26.5m in diameter) in the colonnaded supporting walls, adding half domes to the west and east and piercing the arched tympanum walls on the other two sides with rows of windows. It may be virtually the same plan as the Haghia Sophia, which was clearly its inspiration, but Sinan makes it his own achievement, especially as the interior is so gloriously austere. İznik tiles are used with great restraint, the marble-clad prayer niche (*mihrab*) and pulpit (*mimber*) are simple in design and

The genius of Sinan

By far the most brilliant and prolific Ottoman architect, Sinan was a Christian by birth. Swept up in the annual *devişirme*, a levy of Christian youth taken into the sultan's service and compelled to convert to Islam, he was trained at the Topkapı Palace. In 1536, Sinan became imperial architect and is responsible for some 81 mosques, 50 theological schools, 32 palaces and numerous other structures, from bridges to hospitals – 321 in total. A devout Muslim and simple family man, he lived on site with his family while the Süleymaniye complex was under construction. He was buried here, aged 97, in a tomb, fittingly, he designed himself.

the painted arabesque panels on the plasterwork muted in colour.

Outside, in the southeastern grounds of the mosque are the *türbe*s or **tombs** of Süleyman the Magnificent and his wife Haseki Hürrem or Roxelana (daily 7am–8pm; free). Süleyman's is an octagonal marble drum with a domed roof; inside is the cenotaph of the greatest Ottoman sultan. Ranged in an L-shape around the southwest and northwest sides of the mosque are *medreses,* a hospital and a caravanserai for travellers – all once integral parts of this great philanthropic complex. The baths built as part of the complex are excellent and open to mixed bathing (**Süleymaniye Hamamı**, Mimar Sinan Cad 20 ☎0212 519 5569, ⌂suleymaniyehamami.com; daily 10am–10pm; bath and scrub packages €44).

Grand Bazaar (Kapalı Çarşı)

MAP P.60, POCKET MAP F7
Beyazıt ⓣ1 Beyazıt or Çemberlitaş ☎0212 519 1248. Mon–Sat 9am–7pm.
Known in Turkish as the Kapalı Çarşı or Covered Bazaar, this great shopping complex was originally built not long after the Ottoman Turkish conquest of the city in 1453, on the site of a Byzantine precursor. Like all bazaars in the Ottoman Empire, it was an open area in the beginning, centred on the *bedesten,* a lockable, covered (usually domed) building where

valuable goods were stored. The commercial hub of the Grand Bazaar comprised two *bedesten*, the İç Bedesten, today containing jewellery and other shops, and the Sandal Bedesteni, not built until the sixteenth century, which was used for storing precious fabrics.

Up to half a million shoppers, both visitors and locals, visit the bazaar daily. If you're unused to Middle Eastern ways it can be a little intimidating, not only because of the importuning of a few of the owners of its four thousand or so shops, but also owing to the maze-like meanderings of the **66 vaulted streets** (the name-plaques of which

Süleymaniye Mosque Complex

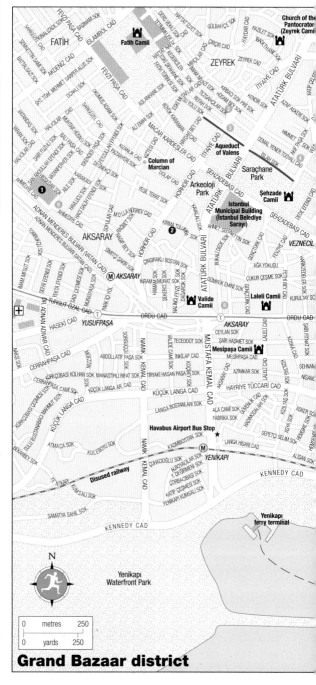

Grand Bazaar district

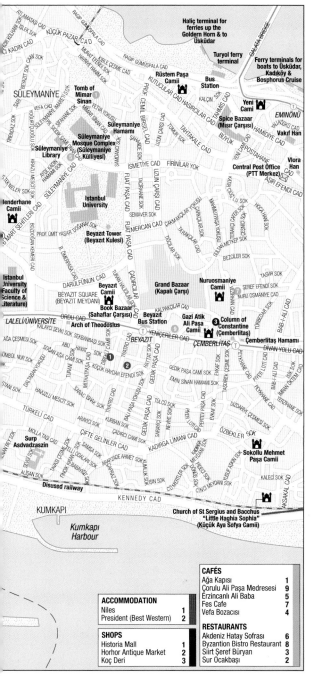

are often hidden beneath displays) and the sheer crush of people at busy times. It's also easy to exit by the "wrong" one of the twenty gates puncturing its walls and end up, disorientated, in an unfamiliar labyinth of alleyways – some of which are still lined by workshops producing goods for the bazaar. In addition to shops, there's a plethora of **cafés and restaurants**, a mosque, moneychangers and banks and, essential given the incredibly high annual turnover in gold here, market police known as *zabita*. Fortunately, the variety of goods on display, from exquisite gold and silver jewellery, antique carpets and flat-weave rugs (kilims) to fake designer clothes and accessories and gaudy belly-dancer outfits, keeps most people entertained, the majority of shop owners pleasant and friendly, and some of the eating places more than reasonable.

Book Bazaar (Sahaflar Çarşısı)

MAP P.60, POCKET MAP E7

Sahaflar Çarşısı Sok ❶ 1 Beyazıt. Daily 9am–7.30pm.

Reachable either from the southwest corner of the Grand Bazaar or from Beyazıt Square, this famous booksellers' market dates back to the Byzantine period. No longer the best place to hunt for secondhand or antiquarian rarities, it concentrates on academic tomes for students from nearby Istanbul University, but has a fair smattering of decent books in English on Istanbul.

Nuruosmaniye Camii

MAP P.60, POCKET MAP F7

Vezirhan Cad ❶ 1 Çemberlitaş.

More or less opposite the Çarşı Kapısı gate on the east side of the Grand Bazaar, this attractive building, built between 1748 and 1755, was the first of the city's

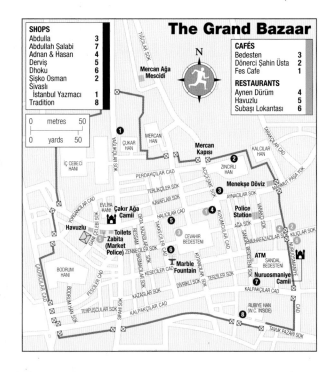

The Grand Bazaar

SHOPS

Abdulla	3
Abdullah Şalabi	7
Adnan & Hasan	4
Derviş	5
Dhoku	6
Şişko Osman	2
Sivaslı İstanbul Yazmacı	1
Tradition	8

CAFÉS

Bedesten	3
Dönerci Şahin Üsta	2
Fes Cafe	1

RESTAURANTS

Aynen Dürüm	4
Havuzlu	5
Subaşı Lokantası	6

Grand Bazaar shopping tips

Few goods bear price labels in the Grand Bazaar, so for most things you'll have to haggle. Before beginning negotiations for a particular item, ask the price of identical or similar items at other stores to give a ball-park figure. Then offer considerably less than the trader is asking (he'll likely be asking far more than he will accept). Walking away is a tactic that sometimes produces results but remember that once you've begun to bargain seriously it is rude not to pursue the process to the end – and not to buy once you've agreed a price is very bad form. The price of gold and silver jewellery fluctuates on a daily basis with prices for items based on the going rate – the jeweller should base his asking price on the weight of the piece you are interested in.

mosques to be influenced by the Baroque style. The prayer hall is little more than an impressively high central dome supported by four great bricked-in arches filled by windows, which flood the interior with light and make its name, the "Sacred Light of Osman", particularly apt. Flanked by twin cylindrical minarets, the mosque has a rare grace, especially as it is fronted by an elegant semicircular, rather than the usual square, courtyard. Due to its proximity to the Grand Bazaar, it is invariably very busy, especially at Friday midday prayers, and its pleasant courtyard, shaded by spreading plane trees, offers a peaceful respite to busy shoppers and workers.

Column of Constantine (Çemberlitaş)

MAP P.60, POCKET MAP F8
Yeniçeriler Cad ⓘ 1 Çemberlitaş.
Rising above all the domed Ottoman buildings hereabouts, this is a reminder of an earlier, Byzantine past, when this 35m-high column presided over the great oval Forum of Constantine. Erected by Constantine to commemorate the inauguration of his new city in 330, it was surmounted by a massive statue of the emperor himself, dressed as Apollo, which was toppled by a storm in 1106. Its Turkish name

Çemberlitaş, or "hooped stone", refers to the reinforcing iron rings clamped around the joints of its ten porphyry drums following an earthquake in 416. It is sometimes called the "burnt column" after it was scorched by a great fire in 1179.

Çemberlitaş Hamamı

MAP P.60, POCKET MAP F8
Vezirhan Cad 8 ⓘ 1 Çemberlitaş ⓦ 0212 522 7974, ⓦ cemberlitashamami.com.tr. Daily 6am–11.30pm. Baths from ₺140.
Opposite the Column of Constantine, this historic

Grand Bazaar

Beyazit Square

bathhouse is one of the three most popular in the old city and well used to foreign visitors. It was founded in the sixteenth century by Nur Banu Valide Sultan. An Italian by birth, she had been seized from the Greek island of Paros and brought to Istanbul to be a concubine in the *harem*. Eventually she ended up as consort to Selim II (1566–74) and mother to Sultan Murat III (1574–95). It follows the usual pattern of the city's Ottoman hamams and certainly makes an atmospheric and very conveniently located introduction to the Turkish bath ritual.

Gazi Atik Ali Paşa Camii

MAP P.60, POCKET MAP F8
Yeniçeriler Cad ● 1 Çemberlitaş.
Often overlooked in favour of more imposing rivals such as the Blue and Süleymaniye mosques, the Gazi Atik Ali Paşa Camii, located a short way west along the tramline from the Column of Constantine, is important, as it is one of Istanbul's oldest mosques. Constructed in 1496 by a eunuch who became grand vizier and whose name the mosque bears, it

consists of a 12m-diameter dome seated on the walls of the main body of the prayer hall, extended by a semi-dome covering another section of the mosque containing the Mecca-facing *mihrab*.

Beyazit Square (Beyazıt Meydanı)

MAP P.60, POCKET MAP E7
Ordu Cad ● 1 Beyazıt.
Flanked to the west by the Grand Bazaar, to the south by traffic-filled Ordu Caddesi and to the north by the grounds of Istanbul University, this large square is one of the few (relatively speaking in this congested city) oases of peace in central Istanbul. The imperial mosque that gives the square its name, the **Beyazıt Camii**, was completed in 1506, making it the second oldest imperial mosque in the city. It's splendidly austere in style, with the usual colonnades ranged around three sides of the courtyard, supported by pillars of fine marble and centred on a pretty, octagonal ablutions fountain. The prayer hall of the mosque is exactly the same dimensions as the courtyard, making for a pleasing

symmetry, and the central dome is abutted to the west and east by semi-domes, giving it the same spacious feel as the Haghia Sophia and Süleymaniye Camii. Walking northwest across the pigeon-filled square, you soon come to the massive, ornamental gate of Istanbul University, one of the most prestigious in Turkey. Visible beyond it, in the grounds, is a striking white building, the **Beyazıt Tower** (Beyazıt Kulesi in Turkish), erected in 1828, which once served as a fire watchtower. The **Museum of Calligraphy**, housed in an Ottoman-era *medrese* in the northwest corner of the square, has been closed for many years. On the south side of the tramline and busy main road from the southwest corner of the square is a tangle of fallen columns, relief-carved with striking tear-drop motifs. This is all that remains of the once-monumental **Arch of Theodosius**, a triumphal arch that spanned the main road into the city centre, and marking the western entrance to what was once the largest forum or public space in Constantinople, the Forum of Theodosius I (379–395).

Laleli Camii

MAP P.60, POCKET MAP D7

Şehzade Camii

Ordu Cad ⓣ 1 Aksaray.

It's worth continuing west from Beyazıt Square down traffic-clogged Ordu Caddesi to see the attractively ornate Laleli Camii, a mosque built in the Ottoman Baroque style between 1759 and 1763, during the reign of Mustafa II. As an imperial mosque, it used to be surrounded by a number of other buildings which served the surrounding community. The most obvious survivor of these is the attractive *sebil* or street fountain, which once dispensed water to the local populace. The mosque's graceful Baroque curves are best viewed from the exterior, but step inside to admire the plethora of columns supporting the main dome and galleries.

Şehzade Camii

MAP P.60, POCKET MAP D6

Şehzadebaşı Cad ⓣ 1 Laleli/Üniverside Ⓜ 2 Vezneciler.

This, the Mosque of the Prince, is named in honour of Prince Mehmet, eldest son of Süleyman the Magnificent, who died in 1543 at the tender age of 21. It's another work of Sinan, and although most experts do not rate it as among his best, for the average visitor it is one of

the most attractive – at least when viewed from the outside. Completed in 1548, the interior is very plain, with a central dome supported by four piers flanked by four semi-domes, giving it a trefoil plan. Outside, the courtyard is very satisfying aesthetically, with the porticoes surrounding all four sides roofed with a total of 16 small domes. But it's the twin minarets that really catch the eye, with their ribbing and low-relief-carved geometric patterns.

Istanbul Municipality Building (İstanbul Belediye Sarayı)

MAP P.60, POCKET MAP D7
Şehzadebaşı Cad ⊕ 1 Laleli/Üniversite.

Important as the first International Modern building in the old city, the design for this 1950s classic was by architect Nevzat Erol. Comprising a typical modernist-style eight-storey office block with a grid facade raised on columns, it is fronted by a meeting hall-cum-reception area surmounted by an unusual cross-arched roof. It may be at odds with its ancient surroundings, but it is certainly striking.

Aqueduct of Valens

MAP P.60, POCKET MAP C6–D6
Atatürk Bulvarı ⊕ 1 Aksaray Ⓜ 2 Vezneciler.

Spanning traffic-clogged Atatürk Bulvarı in two-tiered, 18.5m-high splendour, this aqueduct was in use from its construction around 375 under Emperor Valens through to the nineteenth century. Water was brought from various sources outside the city, piped under the land walls and all the way to the fourth hill, where a major valley between it and the third hill (where the Süleymaniye mosque complex now stands) meant a raised aqueduct was needed – the splendid construction you see today. From a storage reservoir near Beyazıt Square the water was distributed throughout the city. It's possible to follow its ever-decreasing height west from Atatürk Bulvarı to near the **Kalenderhane Camii** (see page 58), perhaps pausing for unusual refreshments at the wonderful *Vefa Bozacısı* (see page 70) en route.

Aqueduct of Valens

Shops: Grand Bazaar

Abdulla

MAP P.62, POCKET MAP F7
Halıcılar Cad 53 ⊕ 1 Beyazıt or Çemberlitaş
⊕ 0212 527 3684, ⓦ abdulla.com. Mon–Sat
9am–7pm.

The fixed prices make this a
popular bet with visitors, drawn in
by the elegant displays of scarves,
pastel-coloured cotton bath wraps,
plump traditional towels, mohair
rugs and all manner of handmade
olive-oil soaps.

Abdullah Şalabi

MAP P.62, POCKET MAP F7
Cevahir Bedesteni 143–151 ⊕ 1 Beyazıt or
Çemberlitaş ⊕ 0212 520 2250. Mon–Sat
9am–7pm.

Great little antiques stall established
in 1880, stocking a wide range
of curios and presided over by
knowledgeable English-speaker Pol
Şalabi. One speciality is icons.

Adnan & Hasan

MAP P.62, POCKET MAP F7
Halıcılar Cad 89–92 ⊕ 1 Beyazıt
or Çemberlitaş ⊕ 0212 527 9887,
ⓦ www.adnanandhasan.com. Mon–Sat
9am–6.30pm.

Long-established carpet and kilim
purveyor stocking everything from
very expensive Hereke carpets to
moderately priced Anatolian and
Caucasian kilims.

Derviş

MAP P.62, POCKET MAP F7
Keseciler Cad 51 ⊕ 1 Beyazıt or
Çemberlitaş ⊕ 0212 528 7883, ⓦ www.
dervis.com. Mon–Sat 9am–7pm.

Choose from a well-displayed
array of silk scarves, cotton bath
towels and robes, pashmina scarves,
natural soaps and, more unusually,
antique kaftans from Central Asia.

Dhoku

MAP P.62, POCKET MAP F7
Takkeciler Sok 52–60 ⊕ 1 Beyazıt or

Adnan & Hasan

Çemberlitaş ⊕ 0212 527 6841. Mon–Sat
9am–7pm.

The concept is contemporary
ethnic, hence the beautiful range
of flat-weave kilims with strikingly
modern geometric designs which
often look far better at home than
more traditional rugs.

Koç Deri

MAP P.60, POCKET MAP F7
Tavuk Pazarı Sk 27 ⊕ 1 Beyazıt or
Çemberlitaş ⊕ 0212 527 5533. Mon–Sat
9am–7pm.

Leather goods are as traditionally
Turkish in origin as carpets and
İznik pottery, and this place sells
some of the best-quality jackets,
bags and other accessories in
the city.

Şişko Osman

MAP P.62, POCKET MAP F7
Zincirli Han ⊕ 1 Beyazıt or Çemberlitaş
⊕ 0212 528 3548, ⓦ siskoosman.com.
Mon–Sat 9am–6pm.

A rambling store presided over by
the knowledgeable and voluble
Şişko (Fat) Osman, stocking all
manner of antique carpets and
kilims. Come here for apple tea and
an entertaining soft-sell.

Sivaslı Istanbul Yazmacı

MAP P.62, POCKET MAP F7

Yağlıkcılar Cad ⓣ 1 Beyazıt or Çemberlitaş
ⓣ 0212 526 7748. Mon–Sat 9am–7pm.

This textile cornucopia, sometimes known as Necdet Danış, has been making quality *peştemals* (Turkish bath towels), tablecloths and scarves, as well as stunning fabrics, for over 40 years. Well regarded by locals for quality goods at fair prices.

Tradition

MAP P.62, POCKET MAP F7

Rubiye Han 11/12, Kürçüler Sok ⓣ 0212 520 7907. Mon–Sat 9am–7pm.

Opened in 1988 and co-run by Frenchwoman Florence Heilbron, this excellent establishment has a very good reputation, plenty of repeat customers (including a coterie of French diplomats and politicians) and sells pieces from €50 to €10,000.

Shops: Aksaray

Historia Mall

MAP P.60, POCKET MAP B6

Adnan Menderes Bulvarı. Buses #38, #39, #55EB ⓣ 0212 532 0202, ⓦ www.historia. com.tr. Daily 10am–10pm.

Handily located next to the excellent *Akdeniz Hatay Sofrası* restaurant (see page 70), this shopping mall is tricky to reach (your best bet from Sultanahmet is to take the T1 tram to the Aksaray stop, and then take a fifteen-minute walk). Spread over four floors are international favourites such as Levi and Converse, along with good Turkish fashion outlets like Mavi (selling jeans etc) and Derimod (which specialises in leather). One floor is taken up by a food court.

Horhor Antique Market

MAP P.60, POCKET MAP C7

Yorum Kırık Tulumba Sok 13/22 ⓣ 1 Aksaray ⓣ 0212 525 9977. Daily 10am–8pm.

Out-of-the-way location but easy enough to reach from the Aksaray T1 tramstop, this massive antiques centre has all manner of wares displayed on five floors, much of it stuff imported from Europe in the nineteenth and early twentieth centuries. You'll have to hunt and haggle hard for a real bargain though.

Cafés

Ağa Kapısı

MAP P.60, POCKET MAP E6

Nazir Hizmet Efendi Sok 11 ⓣ 1 Laleli/ Üniversite Ⓜ 2 Vezneciler ⓣ 0212 519 5176, ⓦ facebook.com/AgaKapisi/. Daily 10am–11pm.

If you're visiting the Süleymaniye complex, don't miss this great café hidden on an alley below Sinan's tomb. The views of the Golden Horn and Galata Bridge are as unexpected as they are superb. Try an Ottoman fruit sherbert, Turkish coffee or *gözleme* (₺7–9 depending on filling), a paratha-like bread-round stuffed with cheese or potato, or even a puff on a *nargile* on the upper floor – all usually in the company of students from the university.

Bedesten

MAP P.62, POCKET MAP F7

Cevahir Bedesteni 143–151 ⓣ 1 Çemberlitaş ⓣ 0212 520 2250. Mon–Sat 8.30am–6.30pm.

Tucked away in the Cevahir Bedesteni in the heart of the Grand Bazaar, this well-run and stylish place makes a great spot to rest-up between shopping bouts. Well-priced food is a mix of Turkish (try the yoghurt-drenched Turkish ravioli, *mantı*, for ₺19) and international (brownies and cheesecake) and the coffee is good. The decor is special too, dominated by two giant *alem*, the brass crescent and star finials that adorn mosque domes and minarets.

Çorlulu Ali Paşa Medresesi

Çorulu Ali Paşa Medresesi

MAP P.60, POCKET MAP F7
Ali Baba Türbe Sok Medrese, Yeniçeriler
Cad 36–38 ⊕ 1 Beyazıt ⓘ 0212 528 3785.
Daily 8am–midnight.
Housed in the Çorulu Ali Paşa
Medrese, the *Erenler Çay Bahçesi* is
a great place to stop for a bargain-
priced traditional Turkish *çay* (tea)
sipped from a tiny, tulip-shaped
glass, or to toke on a *nargile*
(water pipe).

Dönerci Şahin Üsta

MAP P.62, POCKET MAP F7
Nuruosmaniye Kılıçlar Sok 7 ⊕ 1
Çemberlitaş ⓘ 0212 526 5297. Mon–Sat
11am–5pm.
Most visitors pass this hole in the
wall, stand-up *döner* kebab joint
thinking it's just another cheap
place dishing up bland, pre-
prepared *döner*s brought in from
outside. It isn't, as the queues of
loyal regulars attest. Enjoy tender
lamb painstakingly layered on
the vertical spit each morning,
grilled to perfection then sliced
onto a small *pide* bread and served
with juicy tomatoes and sumac-
smothered onion – ₺17.

Erzincanlı Ali Baba

MAP P.60, POCKET MAP E6
Sidik Sami Onar Cad 11 ⊕ 1 Laleli/
Üniversite ⓘ 0212 514 5878. Daily
5am–8.30pm.
Overlooking the Süleymaniye
mosque and with tables out on
the "market of the addicts", this is
an ideal lunch stop – especially if
you like the beans (*kuru fasulye*)
which have made it famous. Tender,
buttery, dripping with tomato sauce
and topped by a spicy pepper, a bowl
of these cheap (₺6) and delicious
pulses is a delight. They also do a
range of other Turkish dishes.

Fes Cafe

MAP P.62, POCKET MAP F7
Ali Baba Türbe Sok 25/7A, off
Nuruosmaniye Cad ⊕ 1 Çemberlitaş
ⓘ 0212 528 1613, ⓦ www.fescafe.com.
Daily 9am–7pm.
Just outside the Grand Bazaar
and with a smaller branch
inside on Halıcılar Cad 62, this
contemporary take on a traditional
Turkish café serves up good
sandwiches and cakes to a mainly
middle-class Turkish clientele. Also
does very decent coffee.

Fes Cafe

Vefa Bozacısı

MAP P.60, POCKET MAP D6
Katip Çeşebi Cad 104/1 ⓘ 1 Laleli/
Üniversite Ⓜ 2 Vezneciler ⓘ 0212
519 4922, ⓦ www.vefa.com.tr. Daily
8am–11.30pm.

Whether you like the traditional
speciality *boza*, a viscous
fermented millet drink topped by
connoisseurs with roasted chickpeas
(bought from a shop across the
road), is almost beside the point,
as the ambience of the delightful
interior is what counts. Caught in
an early twentieth-century time-
warp, it's all dark-wood shelves
and cut-glass mirrors. Slightly
sweet and fizzy, *boza* (₺3 a glass) is
delicious – Atatürk himself thought
so and the glass he drank from in
the 1930s is proudly on display on
one wall. You can also stock up on
chunky souvenir bottles of *nar suyu*
(pomegranate syrup) and *üzüm
sirkesi* (grape vinegar).

Restaurants

Akdeniz Hatay Sofrası

MAP P.60, POCKET MAP B6
Ahmediye Cad 44/A. Buses #38, #55/EB

ⓘ 0212 531 3333. Mon–Sat 8am–midnight.
Unpromisingly located place
specializing in the Arab-
influenced food of the Syrian-
border province of Hatay, this is
nonetheless one of the city's best
restaurants. There's an extensive
range of *meze* ranging from *zahter*,
a thyme-based salad, to *hummus*
topped by *pastırma* (pastrami)
or pine nuts, and spectacular
mains like *tuzda tavuk*, a whole
chicken stuffed with fragrant pilaf
rice, oven-roasted in a thick salt
coating and brought to the table
flaming. Just as ostentatiously
delicious are the metre-long
kebabs. Unlicensed.

Bysantion Bistro Restaurant

MAP P.60, POCKET MAP C7
Selim Paşa Sok 10 ⓘ Aksaray ⓘ 0212 522
7496. Daily 11am–1am.
Located slightly away from the
main attractions of the area, this
restaurant is closer to a few lesser-
known mosques that are still worth
a visit. This place boasts genuinely
friendly staff, and the food won't
disappoint, even if the interior isn't
too elaborate.

Aynen Dürüm

MAP P.62, POCKET MAP F7
Muhafazacilar Sok 33 🚇 Yeniçeriler
☎ 0212 527 4728. Daily 11am–1am.

If you prefer a quick bite to go, grab a sandwich at this little gem. Both locals and tourists queue here and sit at a street pew with a kebab wrap in hand. The liver sandwich is top, but any type of meat you choose is delicious. The quality speaks for itself – this is street food at its best. Definitely worth the wait.

Havuzlu

MAP P.62, POCKET MAP F7
Gani Çelebi Sok 3 🚇 1 Çemberlitaş ☎ 0212 527 3346, 🌐 www.havuzlurestaurant.com. Mon–Sat 11am–7pm.

Brisk-bordering-brusque service is the order of the day in this Grand Bazaar institution, appreciated by locals for its good-quality kebabs (from ₺30) and hearty stews and by visitors for the atmospheric dining room beneath a four-hundred-year-old vaulted ceiling. Choose from over twenty varieties of *sulu yemek* (stew-type dishes) laid out in a giant steamtray and changing daily, with desserts including *sutlaç* (oven-baked rice pudding) and *kabak tatlısı* (candied pumpkin). Unlicensed.

Siirt Şeref Büryan

MAP P.60, POCKET MAP E6
İtfaiye Cad 4. Bus #38 ☎ 0212 635 8085. Mon–Fri 8am–midnight, Sat & Sun 10am–11pm.

Nestling in the shadow of the Aqueduct of Valens, this is the place to try the eastern Turkish speciality *büryan*, lamb cooked slowly in a clay *tandır* oven or, even better, *perde pilaf* (₺15), a delicious rice dish flavoured with almonds, shredded chicken, raisins and spices. Most of the food shops on the fascinating street on which it stands are run by Kurds from the southeast of Turkey and stock all manner of cheeses, spices and other goodies. Unlicensed.

Subaşı Lokantası

MAP P.62, POCKET MAP F7
Nuruosmaniye Cad 48, Çarşı Kapı 🚇 1 Çemberlitaş ☎ 0212 522 4762. Mon–Sat 7am–6pm.

Packed with traders from the Grand Bazaar at lunchtimes, this spit-and-sawdust *lokanta* (traditional Turkish restaurant) dishes up cheap and cheerful stews (from ₺15) from huge steamtrays as well as *köfte* and kebabs. It's conveniently located right outside the main, Çarşı, gate to the bazaar. Unlicensed.

Sur Ocakbaşı

MAP P.60, POCKET MAP C6
İtfaiye Cad 27, Fatih Bus #38 ☎ 0212 533 8088, 🌐 surocakbasi.com. Daily 10am–1am.

Fronting a lively pedestrianised square, this down-to-earth *ocakbaşı* is noted for its *saç tava*, a rich fried meat and vegetable stew usually eaten with copious chunks of *pide* flatbread, as well a startling array of kebabs, spicy *lahmacun* and even the stuffed intestine speciality *bumbar*. TV chef and food personality Anthony Bourdain was brought here when he visited the city.

Havuzlu

Northwest quarter and the land walls

Compelling yet seldom visited, the northwest quarter stands astride the fourth, fifth and sixth hills of the old city. Best explored on foot, its narrow streets, the most evocative running steeply down to the shores of the Golden Horn beneath strings of washing hung between once grand nineteenth-century apartments, are the beat of skullcapped conservative Muslim men and veiled women. Yet working churches survive, including the spiritual centre of the Orthodox Christian world, the Fener Greek Patriarchate, as well as Byzantine treasures like St Saviour in Chora, today the Kariye Museum, with its stunning mosaics and frescoes. The quarter is bounded to the northwest by the remarkably intact fifth-century land walls of Theodosius which, if followed south, run through yet more atmospheric districts dotted with interesting sights, finally ending by the coruscating waters of the Sea of Marmara.

Kariye Museum (Kariye Müzesi)

MAP P.74, POCKET MAP A2
Kariye Camii Sok ⓂⓂ **1 Ulubatlı/Topkapı, buses #28, #36/V, #37/Y, #38, #38/E, #55/ EB, #87** ☎ **0212 631 9241. Daily mid-April– Oct 9am–7pm; Nov–mid-April 9am–5pm. ₺30, audio-guide ₺10.**

Out by the land walls of Theodosius, some 5km from the centre of the old city, the Byzantine **Church of St Saviour in Chora** was converted into a mosque, the Kariye Camii, after the Ottoman conquest. Today, as the **Kariye Museum**, it is the one absolute must-see historic site beyond Sultanahmet and its environs. Possibly dating back to the fourth century, it originally lay beyond the walls of Constantinople – hence "Chora", Greek for "in the country" – but the pretty brick-built building you see today dates largely from an eleventh-century rebuild followed, in the early fourteenth century,

by a remodelling by prominent Byzantine statesman and scholar, **Theodore Metochites**. Crucially, the wealthy Metochites added the twin narthexes (entrance vestibules) and the funerary chapel (parecclesion) to the church, home to the bulk of the mosaics and frescoes which make it so stunning.

You enter the church via a door in the north wall, but to get your bearings, head straight for the outer narthex. The door in the external wall here is today's exit, but was originally the main entrance to the church. Above this door the *Virgin and Angels* mosaic shows Mary with an infant Christ in a medallion on her chest, flanked by two angels. Opposite, above the door to the inner narthex, another panel shows *Christ Pantocrator* or Christ the all-powerful. Running around the entire outer narthex and part of the parecclesion is a narrative sequence of twelve semicircular mosaic panels known as the *Infancy of Christ*, telling the story of Jesus from his birth to his entry into Jerusalem. The second narrative sequence, *Christ's Ministry*, some fifteen scenes spread over the vaults of the roof, begins in the outer narthex before spilling over into part of the inner narthex. Look out for Christ healing a leper covered in almost comic-book-like spots, and the *Miracle at Cana*. On the north wall of the inner narthex, a third wonderful sequence begins, the *Life of the Virgin Mary*, taken from the apocryphal Gospel of St James, which can be traced around the inner narthex from Joachim praying in the wilderness to the miraculous pregnancy of Mary. The twin domes of the inner narthex are filled with the *Genealogy of Christ*, while above the door to the nave, an accomplished mosaic panel shows a wonderfully turbanned Theodore Metochites presenting a model of his church to Christ, flanked by two more mosaics depicting St Peter and St Paul. The nave is notable for its fine marble panels and mosaic of the *Dormition of the Virgin*, but don't leave without

admiring the frescoes in the funerary chapel. Pick of these is the *Resurrection*, with Christ smashing down the doors of hell and rescuing Adam and Eve from their tombs, a painting every bit as brilliantly vibrant as those of the (unknown) artist's Renaissance contemporary, Giotto.

Rezan Has Museum and Gallery (Rezan Has Müzesi)

MAP P.74, POCKET MAP D4
Kadir Has Üniversitesi. Bus #99, #99A & #99Y ⓜ 2 Haliç ⓣ 0212 533 6532, ⓦ rhm. org.tr. Daily 9am–6pm. ₺5.

This museum-cum-exhibition space is housed in Kadir Has University, once a nineteenth-century tobacco factory. A must for archeology buffs, a series of cases exhibit exquisite finds from the Neolithic period through to the Selçuk Turkish era, atmospherically set out in a Byzantine cistern in the bowels of the university. The artefacts are mainly Anatolian and superb examples of their type – from Urartian metalwork to Hellenistic-era surgical equipment, seal stones to Roman figurines. The

Frescoes in Kariye Museum

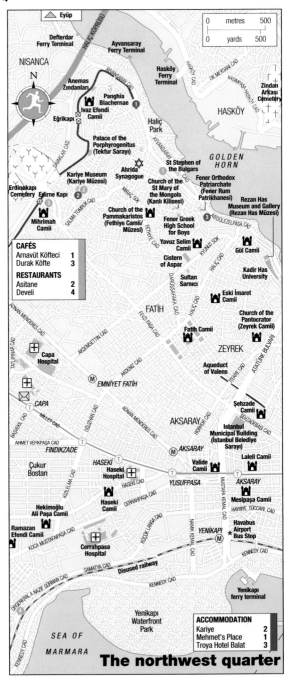

The northwest quarter

adjoining gallery hosts a mixed bag of exhibitions.

Church of the Pantocrator (Zeyrek Camii)

MAP P.74, POCKET MAP D5
İbadethane Sok, İtfaiye Cad. Buses #28, #28/T.

Converted into a mosque after the Ottoman conquest, this fine late-Byzantine building stands on a hilltop above Atatürk Bulvarı. Built in 1136, it comprised two churches linked by a chapel. The interior retains some fine marble panels and opus sectile flooring of differently coloured marble pieces. A short walk southwest is the Kadınlar Pazarı (Women's Bazaar), home to a plethora of food shops run mainly by Kurds.

Fener Greek High School for Boys

MAP P.74, POCKET MAP B3
Sancaktar Yokuşu Sok 36, Fener Bus #99.

This imposing Victorian-Gothic building, built with bricks imported from France in 1883, is an unmissable sight on the slopes of the old city's fifth hill. There has been a school here since Byzantine times but today it's hard not to view it without thinking about the precipitous decline of the Greek minority in the city since its construction. Then there were over 400,000 Greeks in a city with a population of around one million. Today, there are just 2,000 or so in a metropolis of seventeen million; in 2014, fewer than sixty pupils attended this cavernous school.

Fatih Camii

MAP P.74, POCKET MAP C5
İslambol Cad. Buses #28, #28/T, #36/V, #37/Y, #38/E.

Northwest along the line of the aqueduct is the monumental and newly restored Fatih Camii (Mosque of the Conqueror). This impressive structure was Istanbul's first purpose-built (as opposed to a converted church) mosque.

Interior of Fatih Camii

Finished in 1470, it was largely rebuilt after an earthquake in 1776. At the centre of the usual complex, this is the heart of the old city's most conservative district and bearded men in skullcaps are a common sight, as are chador-clad women. On Wednesdays the streets roundabout are home to Istanbul's most vibrant street market, the **Çarşamba Pazarı**.

Yavuz Selim Camii

MAP P.74, POCKET MAP C3
Yavuz Selim Cad. Buses #28, #28/T, #36/V, #37/Y, #38/E.

This austerely beautiful mosque lies northwest of the Fatih Camii, on the fifth hill. Its shallow single dome spans the prayer hall with sublime simplicity and İznik tiles are used with great restraint. Almost as impressive as the mosque are the splendid views from the attractive grounds, down over the Golden Horn and beyond. Behind the mosque the **tomb of Selim the Grim** (daily except Tues 9am–4.30pm; **₺2**) is worth a look, as he was arguably the most successful Ottoman sultan, adding parts of Persia plus Syria, Palestine,

Arabia and Egypt to the empire. He was known as "the Grim" for his habit of chopping off the heads of unsatisfactory grand viziers on a regular basis. The tomb retains a couple of superb tile panels.

The large, square hollow as you approach Yavuz Selim Camii used to function as the early Byzantine **Cistern of Aspar**, an open cistern once the largest of its kind in the city. Its brick-built retaining walls are still partially visible. Also nearby, down narrow Ali Naki Sokak, is the **Sultan Sarnıcı**. This beautiful, covered **Byzantine cistern** is some 29m by 19m and has a brick-vaulted ceiling supported by marble pillars, each topped by a richly sculpted Corinthian capital. The cistern, now completely dry, functions as an atmospheric venue for wedding receptions and the like. It is usually open 9am–6pm, and entry is free.

Church of the Pammakaristos (Fethiye Camii/Müzesi)

MAP P.74, POCKET MAP B3
Fethiye Cad. Bus #28. Daily April–Oct 9am–7pm; Nov–March 9am–5pm. t5.

Overshadowed by the nearby Kariye Museum (see page 72), the **mosaics** in the funerary chapel of **the former Church of the Pammakaristos** are one of the "hidden" treasures of the city. The church was converted into a mosque in the late sixteenth century and still functions as one today, but the former chapel containing the mosaics has been turned into the **Fethiye Museum**. The typically brick-built domed building of the Byzantine church dates back to the twelfth century, while the chapel containing the mosaics was added in 1310. Well signed, the superbly preserved and vibrant mosaics include Christ Pantocrator in the dome, surrounded by the twelve Prophets, and a baptism scene showing Christ and John the Baptist. Between 1456 and 1587, this church was the Greek Orthodox Patriarchate.

Church of St Mary of the Mongols (Kanlı Kilisesi)

MAP P.74, POCKET MAP C3
Tevkii Cafer Mektebi Sok. Bus #99.
Reached either from the fifth hill above or the shores of the Golden

Fethiye Camii/Müzesi

St Stephen of the Bulgars

Horn in Fener below, the unusual thirteenth-century Church of St Mary of the Mongols, in the shadow of the massive Fener Greek High School for Boys, is well worth a look. It's the only church in the city where Orthodox services have been carried out from the Byzantine period to the present day, but entry is dependent on the caretaker being at home.

Fener Orthodox Patriarchate (Fener Rum Patrikhanesi)

MAP P.74, POCKET MAP C3
Mursel Paşa Cad. Bus #99 ☎ 0212 525 2117. Daily 9am–5pm. Free.
On level ground close to the Golden Horn waterfront and stretches of the Byzantine sea walls that once ringed the peninsula and joined up with the land walls (see page 79), the Greek Orthodox Patriarchate remains, at least in theory, the spiritual centre of Orthodox Christians worldwide. The **Church of St George** at the heart of the complex, built in 1720, has a barrel-vaulted ceiling, an excess of gilt but one particularly fine portable mosaic icon of the Virgin Mary.

St Stephen of the Bulgars

MAP P.74, POCKET MAP C2
Murel Paşa Cad 85–88. Bus #99. Daily 8am–5pm. Free.
Stranded on a traffic island close to the waterfront, this church was constructed from cast-iron panels in Vienna in the late nineteenth century and floated down the Danube into the Black Sea and thence on to Istanbul. With its golden domes, it's very attractive, especially when viewed from the Haliç ferry. Major restoration started in 2013 and ended in 2017.

Ahrida Synagogue

MAP P.74, POCKET MAP B2
Kürkçüçeşme Sok. Bus #99 ☎ 0212 243 5166. Contact the Chief Rabbinate at least one day before to arrange a visit. Free.
Hidden away in the backstreets of the atmospheric district of Balat, once home to a sizeable Jewish community, this originally fifteenth-century synagogue was rebuilt in Baroque style in 1694. The Jews have long since moved to other parts of the city or

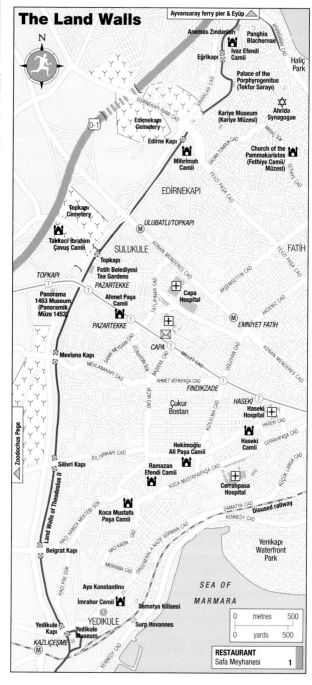

The Land Walls

Ayvansaray ferry pier & Eyüp

Anemas Zındanları
Panghia Blachernae
Eğrikapı
Ivaz Efendi Camii
Haliç Park
Palace of the Porphyrogenitus (Tekfur Sarayı)
Kariye Museum (Kariye Müzesi)
Ahrida Synagogue
Edirnekapı Cemetery
Edirne Kapı
Church of the Pammakaristos (Fethiye Camii/ Müzesi)
Mihrimah Camii
EDİRNEKAPI
FATİH
Topkapı Cemetery
ULUBATLI/TOPKAPI
Takkeci İbrahim Çavuş Camii
SULUKULE
Topkapı
Fatih Belediyesi Tea Gardens
TOPKAPI
PAZARTEKKE
Panorama 1453 Museum (Panoramik Müze 1453)
Ahmet Paşa Camii
Çapa Hospital
PAZARTEKKE
EMNİYET FATİH
CAPA
Mevlana Kapı
FINDIKZADE
Çukur Bostan
HASEKİ
Haseki Hospital
Silivri Kapı
Hekimoğlu Ali Paşa Camii
Haseki Camii
Ramazan Efendi Camii
Cerrahpaşa Hospital
Disused railway
Koca Mustafa Paşa Camii
Belgrat Kapı
Yenikapı Waterfront Park
Aya Konstantino
İmrahor Camii
SEA OF MARMARA
Samatya Kilisesi
YEDİKULE
Surp Hovannes
Yedikule Kapı
Yedikule Museum
KAZLIÇEŞME

Land Walls of Theodosius II

Zoodochus Pege

| 0 | metres | 500 |
| 0 | yards | 500 |

| RESTAURANT | |
| Safa Meyhanesi | 1 |

Land walls of Theodosius

This superb feat of Byzantine engineering stretches some 6.5km, from the Sea of Marmara to the Golden Horn, thus cutting off the peninsula on which the city was built from the rest of Europe – and it kept foes as formidable as **Attila the Hun** and the Arab armies of Islam at wall's-width for a thousand years. Constructed as a single wall in 413 under Theodosius II, following a disastrous earthquake in 447 the defences were rebuilt in triplicate. The inner wall of the defences was now 5m thick and 12m high, strengthened by 96 towers; the outer wall 2m by 8.5m, again fortified by towers spaced between those on the main wall behind; in front lays a 20m-wide moat. **Walking** the line of the walls today is an adventure, with opportunities to mount the battlements and visit a number of other sights en route. Avoid leaving late in the day as the wall runs through poor neighbourhoods, and petty theft is not unknown around dusk and after dark.

To get to the south end of the walls at Yedikule, take the #80 bus from Eminönü or the #80/T from Taksim. Much easier is to take the Marmaray metro from Sirkeci to the Kazlıçeşme stop, just outside the walls near Yedikule. From the north end of the walls, the Haliç ferry runs down the Golden Horn from Ayvansaray to Eminönü, or take the #99 bus to the same destination.

migrated to Israel, but it receives a fair number of visitors despite the problems of having to arrange a visit in advance.

Yedikule Museum

MAP P.78
Kale Meydanı Cad. ⊙ 1 train, buses #80, #80/T. ☏ 0212 585 8933. Tues–Sun 8.30am–6pm. ₺10.

Wall-walking enthusiasts should start where the wall began, at the **Marble Tower** on the south side of traffic-filled Kennedy Caddesi. A short walk north on the outside of the walls is **Yedikule Gate** (Yedikule Kapı). Enter here as access to Yedikule Museum is on the inside of the walls. Essentially a fortress added to the line of the Byzantine walls by Mehmet the Conqueror in 1457–58, it consists of three large towers linked by a curtain wall and connected to a section of the land walls which boasts four towers of its own. This gives rise to the fortification's Turkish name Yedikule, "The Seven Towers". Yedikule was, ironically given its appearance, never used as a fort. Two of its towers left of the entrance were in Ottoman times a prison and treasury, and the section of land walls incorporates the earlier, famous **Golden Gate**. This triple-arched structure, now bricked up, was a triumphal arch erected under Theodosius I in 390 over one of the main roads leading into Constantinople.

Belgrat Kapı

MAP P.78
Bus #93/T.

From **Yedikule Kapı**, it's possible to follow the outside of the partially restored walls northwards. The moat is now used for market gardens, but there are well-preserved sections of outer and inner wall. The next gate, **Belgrat (Belgrade) Kapı**, was originally a military gate that included portals through the inner and outer walls but did not have – as the public gates had – a bridge across the moat.

Panaroma 1453 Museum

Zoodochus Pege
Balikli Kilise

Seyit Nizam Cad 3. Bus #93/T. Daily 8.30am–4.30pm. Free.

Following the walls north you reach **Silivri Kapı**, known as Pege in Byzantine times because of the nearby shrine of **Zoodochus Pege**. Cross the busy six-lane highway paralleling the walls and follow a road 500m west through mixed Muslim and Christian cemeteries to a pretty nineteenth-century Greek church, built over a much earlier Byzantine structure. It's famed for the fish living in its *ayazma*, a sacred underground spring.

Panorama 1453 Museum (Panoramik Müze1453)

MAP P.78

Topkapı Kültür Parkı 1 Topkapı ☎ 0212 415 1453, ⓦ panoramikmuze.com. Daily 8am–5pm. ₺15, audio-guide ₺5.

North of Silivri Kapı is Mevlana Kapı. Northwest of this gate, across the six-lane highway in an area of urban park stranded in a major junction, is the Panorama 1453 Museum. Turks outnumber foreigners here, no doubt because the museum glorifies the iconic conquest of what was then Christian Constantinople by the Muslim, Ottoman Turks on 29 May 1453. Downstairs a circular viewing gallery runs beneath a large dome on which is cleverly painted – in an eye-boggling 360-degree panorama – the army of the young Sultan Mehmet I besieging the walls of Constantinople. Flaming balls of Greek fire, the Byzantines' "secret" weapon, pour down on the hapless attackers, who hold the green flag of Islam aloft in defiance, and the mighty walls crack and crumble under the assault of the Orban, a monster cannon over 8m long and with a bore wide enough to allow a man to crawl inside. The impressive scene, reputed to contain over 10,000 figures, is enhanced by a realistic battlefield tableau ringing the viewing gallery.

The Walls – Topkapı to Edirne Kapı

MAP P.78

Back across the busy thoroughfare from the Panorama 1453 Museum and on the north side of Millet

Caddesi, which runs either side of the T1 tramline, is the Topkapı or **Gate of the Cannonball**, named after the Orban cannon that pulverized the land walls with shot weighing up to half a tonne. Continuing north you have to negotiate traffic-choked Adnan Menderes (Vatan) Caddesi – preferably by the underpass that also leads to the M1 Ulubatlı/Topkapı stop. Between here and Edirne Kapı is a pronounced dip, the valley of the Lycus river, a weak point because the walls along the valley floor were lower than the besiegers' weaponry. This is where the Turks finally and decisively pierced the walls and poured into the city. The walls now run through Sulukule, a neighbourhood home to a **gypsy community** for centuries. Many of the traditional wood houses they inhabited have been controversially bulldozed by the municipality, with posh villas in walled compounds put in their place.

Mihrimah Camii

MAP P.78
Edirnekapı. Buses #28, #36/V, #37/Y, #38, #38/E, #55/EB.

Majestically located on the summit of the sixth of the old city's seven hills, this recently restored mosque is one of architect Sinan's (see page 59) earlier masterpieces. It was commissioned by Rüstem Paşa, grand vizier to Süleyman the Magnificent, and his wife Mihrimah, the sultan's favourite daughter. Access is via steps on the north side of the mosque. The beautiful prayer hall is incredibly light and airy due to the three rows of windows puncturing each of the four filled arches supporting the 20m-diameter dome. Just beyond the Mihrimah Camii is **Edirne Kapı** which bears, on the outside, a modern plaque in Turkish proclaiming it the entry point of the victorious Sultan Mehmet II on 29 May 1453.

Palace of the Porphyrogenitus (Tekfur Sarayı)

MAP P.74, POCKET MAP A2
Edirnekapı, Şişhane Cad. Buses #28, #36/V, #37/Y, #38, #38/E, #55/EB.

The walls dip down towards the Golden Horn past Edirne Kapı. Built into the line, well-preserved here, is the **Tekfur Saray,** or **Palace of the Porphyrogenitus**. Until 2014 a mere shell, this former annexe of the Blachernae Palace has been controversially rebuilt as a congress and exhibition centre. The palace marks the start of a change in the walls, now a single, thicker line bulging out to the west and running down the steep hill towards the Golden Horn, built in the seventh century.

Eyüp Camii

Cami Kebir Sok. Buses #99, #39, or Haliç ferry.

A short walk north of the land walls is the district of Eyüp, named after Eyüp Ensari, standard bearer of the Prophet Mohammed, who died and was buried here during the first Arab siege of Constantinople (674–78). At

Mihrimah Camii

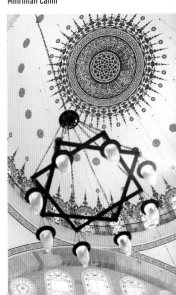

the heart of the area the mosque bearing the standard bearer's name, and his tomb, stand opposite each other across a courtyard – usually thronged with pilgrims. The mosque dates back to 1458 but was rebuilt in Baroque style in 1800 following an earthquake. The tomb (Tues–Sun 9.30am–4.30pm; free) itself is covered in an eclectic mix of fine tiles. This is a sacred spot for Muslims – arguably the third most important Islamic pilgrimage site after Mecca and Jerusalem – and the whole area very conservative, so make sure you are modestly attired and women cover their heads in both mosque and tomb.

Tomb of Sokollu Mehmet Paşa

Cami Kebir Cad. Buses #99, #39, or Haliç ferry. Tues–Sun 9.30am–4.30pm.

A short way south of Eyüp Camii is a fine tomb, one of the many dotted around here. It houses the remains of Sokollu Mehmet Paşa, a Bosnian who became one of the empire's greatest grand viziers under Süleyman the Magnificent. The work of the leading architect

of the day, Sinan, it was completed in 1574. It's a beautiful work of art, a severe octagonal structure topped by a dome and embellished with some lovely stained glass. The other buildings ranged around it are part of the tomb complex and include a library, *medrese*, Koran school and the tombs of the grand vizier's family.

Eyüp Cemetery

Gümüssuyu Karyağdı Sok. Buses #99, #39, or Haliç ferry.

On the prominent hill north of the mosque and tombs is a Muslim cemetery, thick with cypress trees standing sentinel over Ottoman-era, and much more recent and decidedly less ornate, tombstones. At the top is a very popular tea garden, the *Pierre Loti Café* (daily 8am–midnight), named after the French Romantic novelist who frequented the area in the late nineteenth century. A cable car links the banks of the Golden Horn, some 400m north of the Eyüp ferry quay, to the hilltop café (daily 8am–midnight ₺4).

Tomb of Sokollu Mehmet Paşa

Cafés

Arnavüt Köfteci

MAP P.74, POCKET MAP B2
Mursel Paşa Cad 139. Bus #99. ☎ 0212 531
6652. Daily 6am–4.30pm.

A cult institution on the banks
of the Golden Horn, specializing
in cheap (₺16), tender grilled
Albanian-style meatballs (*köfte*).
The attractive European-style
building dates back to the
nineteenth century when this
was a really cosmopolitan
neighbourhood, the eclectic slew of
formica-topped tables only to the
1950s – just a few years after the
place first opened its doors in 1947.

Durak Köfte

MAP P.74
Mihrimah Sultan Camii Altı 361. Bus #28,
#36/V, #37/Y, #38, #38/E, #55/EB ☎ 0212
587 9868. Daily 10am–6.30pm.

Meatballs are a staple Turkish
fast food and this place does a
Macedonian-style *köfte* along
with a range of other good-value
workers' favourites like *kuru fasulye*
or haricot beans in tomato sauce.
Set beneath the lovely Mihrimah
mosque with a few outside tables.

Restaurants

Asitane

MAP P.74, POCKET MAP A2
Kariye Hotel, Kariye Camii Sok 18 🚇 1
Topkapı/Ulubatlı or buses #28, #36/V,
#37/Y, #38, #38/E, #55/EB ☎ 0212 635
7997, 🌐 asitane.business.site. Daily
noon–10.30pm.

Worth splashing out on, this
restaurant in the chestnut-tree-
shaded courtyard of the *Kariye
Hotel* (see page 137) was one of
the first places to revive Ottoman-
style cuisine, bringing new/old
flavours to foreigners and locals
alike. Try the *hünkar beğendi*
(literally "the sultan liked it"), an
Ottoman classic done to perfection
here. Mains around ₺45. Licensed.

Asitane

Develi

MAP P.74
Gumuş Yüzük Sok 7 🚇 1 Kocamustafapaşa
☎ 0212 529 0833. Daily noon–midnight.

Founded in 1912 by émigrés from
the south of the country, and it
is still sizzling-out some of the
tenderest, tastiest meat (kebabs
from ₺35) in the city. Overlooking
an atmospheric little square, the
top-floor terrace has great views
over the Sea of Marmara. The *meze*
and *baklava* are just as good as the
wide range of kebabs. Licensed.

Safa Meyhanesi

MAP P.78
İlyasbey Cad 12, Yedikule Marmaray
🚇 Kazlıçeşme, ☎ 0212 585 5594. Daily
noon–midnight.

This delightful old school *meyhane*
looks like the stage set for a 1940s
movie, with its wooden walls, high
ceiling and glittering chandelier,
shelves of *rakı* bottles and the
original posters advertising this
potent aniseed spirit. It's a little out
of the way and has no live music so it
appeals to Istanbul intellectuals and
academics out for an evening. *Meze*s
are reasonable at between ₺10–20;
fish of the day is priced by the kilo.

Galata and the waterfront districts

Dominated by the landmark Galata Tower, which takes its name from the vibrant district at its feet, Galata's cobbled alleys tumble down to the busy north shore of the Golden Horn. An autonomous Genoese colony in the late Byzantine era, home to thriving Jewish, Moorish, Armenian and Greek communities since the Ottoman conquest, it has always been different from the conservative, mainly Muslim old city. Over the last decade it has blossomed from a run-down port area to a bohemian quarter of trendy shops, artists' studios, musicians' workshops, street art, hip bars and clubs. A quaint nineteenth-century underground funicular continues to toil up the hill and dervishes still whirl at the Galata Mevlevi Lodge.

Galata Tower (Galata Kulesi)

MAP P.86, POCKET MAP A15
Galata Meydanı ☏ 0212 293 8180. Daily 9am–8.30pm. ₺25.

Best reached by walking down Galip Dede Caddesi from İstiklal Tünel station, this soaring, 61m-high medieval tower, capped by a distinctive conical roof, was known as the Tower of Christ when it was built by the Genoese in 1349. Originally part of the fortification wall constructed to protect the Genoese mercantile colony established within it, it was turned into a jail in the fifteenth century. In the seventeenth century, it was used, successfully according to famous Ottoman traveller Evliya Çelebi, by pioneers experimenting in manned flight. From the eighteenth century, its purpose was more prosaic and pragmatic, as a watchtower for the then all too common fires. It is by far the biggest attraction in Galata, with long queues sometimes snaking around the square – particularly for the ever-popular sunset viewing period. The lookout gallery, reached today by a lift, is often crowded, but the views are worth it, with a foreground of the ferry-filled Golden Horn and manic Eminönü waterfront backed by the serene, mosque-lined skyline of the old city, all stately domes and elegant minarets. The tower is home to an expensive café and touristy oriental floor-shows take place most evenings after 8pm.

Galata Mevlevi Lodge (Galata Mevlevihanesi)

MAP P.86, POCKET MAP A14
Galipdede Cad ☏ 0212 678 0618, ⓦ rumimevlevi.com. Tues–Sun April–Oct 9am–7pm; Nov–March 9am–5pm. ₺10.

This former lodge or monastery (*tekke*) of the Mevlevî Sufi order was home to one of Islam's mystical sects, the Mevlevîs. The order was founded in the thirteenth century by Mevlâna who, tired of the constraints of mainstream Sunni Islam, took his followers down the path of love and acceptance. Mevlâna's disciples, or dervishes, are best known in the West for their hypnotic rotating dance, hence "whirling dervish". This ritual dance, along with prayer, meditation, contemplation and music, enabled adherents to achieve mystical union with God. The Mevlevis, along with all Sufi orders, were deemed reactionaries by Atatürk and, in 1923, banned. The order went "underground" for decades but today is semi-officially tolerated. The lodge, built in the fifteenth century but much remodelled, is now a fascinating museum. Exhibits in the downstairs rooms, reached via a peaceful courtyard/garden area, are arranged clockwise. Here, you can see the traditional instruments that provided the musical accompaniment to the dances, dervish costumes, begging bowls, kitchen utensils and a host of other interesting items. Upstairs is the *semahane*, where the dervishes whirled, a beautifully decorated, high-ceilinged octagonal room where dervish shows for visitors are held most Sundays between April and September at 5pm, twice monthly the rest of the year (₺40).

Ottoman Bank Museum/ SALT Gallery

MAP P.86, POCKET MAP A15
Bankalar Cad 35 ⊙ 0212 334 2200, ⊚ obmuze.com. Tues–Sat noon–8pm, Sun 10.30am–6pm. Free.

Aptly situated on the "Street of Banks" and today owned by one of Turkey's leading banks, Garanti, this grandiose building was once the headquarters of the Ottoman Imperial Bank. The French architect behind this typically nineteenth-century European-style building was Vallaury, who also designed the Archeology Museum (see page 42) and *Pera Palace Hotel* (see page 139). Its cavernous interior has been cleverly modernized for Garanti Bank's **SALT contemporary arts project** and hosts a variety of temporary exhibitions. If the current exhibitions are not to your taste, it's worth perusing the permanent **Ottoman Bank Museum** on the ground floor. The bank served Galata's mainly non-Muslim,

Dervishes, Galata Mevlevi Lodge

GALATA AND THE WATERFRONT DISTRICTS

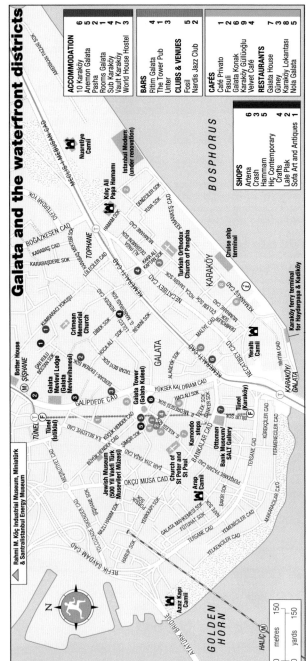

Galata and the waterfront districts

ACCOMMODATION	
10 Karaköy	6
Anemon Galata	5
Pasha	2
Rooms Galata	1
Sub Karaköy	4
Vault Karaköy	7
World House Hostel	3

BARS	
Ritim Galata	4
The Tower Pub	1
Unter	3

CLUBS & VENUES	
Fosil	5
Nardis Jazz Club	2

CAFÉS	
Café Privato	1
Fasuli	2
Galata Konak	6
Karaköy Güllüoğlu	9
Velvet Café	4

RESTAURANTS	
Galata House	7
Güney	3
Karaköy Lokantası	8
Nola Galata	5

SHOPS	
Artena	6
Crash	3
Hammam	5
Hiç Contemporary Crafts	4
Lale Plak	2
Sofa Art and Antiques	1

Greek, Armenian and Jewish inhabitants.

Around Bankalar Caddesi

MAP P.86, POCKET MAP A15

The whole of Bankalar Caddesi is lined with fine, European-style nineteenth- and early twentieth-century buildings. Just west of the Ottoman Bank Museum, the **Kamondo steps**, sinuously curved, Art Nouveau-style twin staircases, were commissioned by the wealthy Jewish Kamondo family in 1860. They achieved iconic status in the 1960s when they were photographed by Henri Cartier-Bresson, a friend of equally accomplished Istanbul-Armenian photographer and local resident Ara Güler. Just off Bankalar Caddesi on Galata Kulesi Sokak, the **Church of St Peter and St Paul** dates back to the fifteenth century and still holds Mass every Sunday. Running parallel to Bankalar Caddesi is Galata Mahkamesi Caddesi, where you'll find the **Arap Camii**. Built as a Genoese church, it was converted into a mosque for the Moorish community in the sixteenth century.

Jewish Museum (500 Yil Vakfi Türk Musevileri Müzesi)

MAP P.86, POCKET MAP A16
Büyük Hendek Cad 39 ☎ 0212 292 6363, ✪ muze500.com. Mon–Thurs 10am–4pm, Fri 10am–1pm, Sun 10am–2pm. ₺10.
Originally housed in the Zulfaris synagogue, the Jewish Museum moved to the larger Neve Shalom synagogue in 2015. Celebrating over five hundred years of Sephardic Jewish culture in Istanbul, the museum is split into three main sections: the first chronicles Jewish history in Anatolia from the fourth century BC onwards; the second is largely ethnographic; and the third has a series of touchscreens on Jewish traditions. Also on site are a café, a shop and an associated museum, that of local Jewish artist.

Kılıç Ali Paşa Hamamı

MAP P.86, POCKET MAP C14
Kılıç Ali Paşa Hamamı Hamam Sok 1 ☎ 1 Tophane ☎ 0212 393 8010, ✪ kilicalipasahamami.com. Daily 8am–4pm (women); 4.30–11.30pm (men), ₺270 including scrub and massage.
Attached to the sixteenth-century Kılıç Ali Paşa mosque, on the north side of Galata bridge, this superb Turkish bathhouse opened in 2013 after a seven-year restoration process. Like the mosque, it's the work of Sinan and is a quite beautiful example of an Ottoman-era hamam (bathhouse), with the brickwork of the domed changing room lovingly exposed, light streaming in through small, star-shaped windows in the dome surmounting the bathing areas.

Getting to, and around, Galata

MAP P.86

Most people coming to Galata from the old city take the T1 tram to the Karaköy stop and walk up into the compact, hillside neighbourhood to see the sights, shop, eat or go to a club. Alternatively, take the nearby late-nineteenth-century underground funicular Tünel (see page 146) to its top, İstiklal station, and walk down. Coming from Taksim Square, the antique tram (see page 146) running down pedestrianized İstiklal Caddesi will save you 1.5km of walking. Coming in from the northern suburbs and Taksim, the M2 metro to Şişhane is useful. All sights and listings in Galata and its immediate environs are best approached in this way, unless otherwise stated, and thence on foot.

Karaköy District

Rahmi M. Koç Industrial Museum

Hasköy Cad 5. Buses #47, #47E, #54/ HT or Haliç ferry to Hasköy pier ☎ 0212 369 6000, Ⓦ www.rmk-museum.org.tr. April–Sept Tues–Fri 10am–5pm, Sat & Sun 10am–8pm; Oct–March 10am–6pm. ₺12.5.

The first and best of three worthwhile and, certainly for Istanbul, unusual sights dotted along the north bank of the Golden Horn. Long a shipbuilding area, part of the museum is appropriately housed in what was, in the eighteenth century, a foundry for ships' chains and anchors. Today, it is home to everything from penny-farthings to Royal Enfield motorcycles, Trabants to Rolls-Royces and a working tram to a model railway. Other highlights include a working ship's bridge, complete with echo sounder and alarm, and a street of period shops and houses. It's the largest collection of industrial-era artefacts in Turkey, the vision of a member of one of Turkey's wealthiest families, and contains a couple of upmarket café-restaurants.

Miniatürk

İmrahor Cad. Buses #47, #47E or #54/HT or Haliç ferry to Sütlüce and walk ☎ 0212 222 2882, Ⓦ miniaturk.com.tr. Daily 9am–6pm. ₺15.

Northwest of the Rahmi M. Koç Industrial Museum, just beyond the massive Haliç bridge, this attraction is a great hit with the locals, displaying a hundred 1:25 scale models of Turkey's most important sights. The majority are buildings, though a couple of geological wonders, Cappadocia's famed fairy chimneys and Pamukkale's travertine terraces, have snuck in. The models are arranged around a near 2km-long signed route in a walled enclosure near the banks of the Golden Horn. If you're pressed for time to see the real thing, here are Istanbul's very own Süleymaniye Mosque, Dolmabahçe Palace and Haghia Sophia – there's even the 1970s Bosphorus Bridge and Atatürk airport.

Santralistanbul Energy Museum

Kazımkarabekir Cad 2. Free bus from Taksim Square, buses #54/HT, #99 or Haliç ferry to Eyüp pier ☎ 0212 311 7878 Ⓦ santralistanbul.org. Daily 9am–6pm. Free; guided tours ₺25 per person.

The furthest of the three Golden Horn attractions from the city centre and right at the head of the inlet, the Energy Museum is housed in a converted power station that began life in 1914 and was for many years the city's sole electricity producer. The Energy Museum has carefully preserved the plant's control room, where a massive bank of dials, switches and gauges helped workers keep control of the giant Siemens engines. Thrown in for good measure is some far more cutting-edge technical wizardry, including a thermal-imaging screen.

Miniatürk

Shops

Artena

MAP P.86, POCKET MAP A15
Camekan Sok 1. ☎ 0212 243 5318. Daily
9am–9.30pm.

Established in 2004, this
designer boutique stocks a range
of handcrafted jewellery, hats
and bags, plus a range of ethnic
artefacts collected from Anatolian
villages and traditional jewellery
from the southeast. You'll likely be
offered tea or coffee as you browse.

Crash

MAP P.86, POCKET MAP A14
Galipdede Cad 35. ☎ 0212 292 4364. Mon–
Sat 9.30am–11pm.

The Galata neo-bohemian's outlet
of choice, this small store stocks
a range of carefully chosen (to be
slightly alt and cool) end-of-line
jeans, shorts, tees, hoodies, dresses
and the like – and knocks them out
at fair prices.

Hammam

MAP P.86, POCKET MAP A15
Kule Çıkmazı. ☎ 0212 245 7075, ⓦ www.
.com.tr. Daily 11am–7pm.

A wide range of Turkish bath
accessories is on offer here, from
quality cotton *peştemal* wraps
to fancy soap bowls, as well as
handmade soaps and lotions – all
presented with panache.

Hiç Contemporary Crafts

MAP P.86, POCKET MAP B14
Lüleci Hendek Sok 35, Karaköy ☎ 0212
251 9973, ⓦ hiccrafts.com. Mon–Sat
11am–7pm.

This small shop specialises in
tasteful furniture and accessories
by local designers. Most items have
an ethnic feel about them, though
they are very contemporary in style.
Look out also for the fine *ikat* and
suzani fabrics from Central Asia.

Lale Plak

MAP P.86, POCKET MAP B14
Galipdede Cad 1. ⓦ facebook.com/
laleplak1/. Mon–Fri 9am–7.30pm, Sat
9am–8pm, Sun noon–7pm.

Located where Galipdede Caddesi
joins throbbing İstiklal Caddesi,
Lale Plak is the Istanbul music-
buffs' store of choice. It was
established over fifty years ago
and leafing through the racks of
jazz and rock vinyl classics is a

Hiç Contemporary Crafts

retro delight, but there's plenty of Turkish and Western music on CD for sale too.

Sofa Art and Antiques

MAP P.86, POCKET MAP B14

Serdar-ı Ekrem Sok 47, Galata ⓣ 0212 520 2850, ⓦ kashifsofa.com. Mon–Sat 9am–7pm.

Established back in 1976 by husband and wife team Kaşif and Dilek, Sofa Art and Antiques is situated on very fashionable Serdar-ı Ekrem street, near the Galata Tower. It is a reputable place to hunt down antiques and vintage items both from Europe and Ottoman Turkey, including calligraphy, tiles, miniatures and textiles. There's another branch in the Grand Bazaar.

Cafés

Café Privato

MAP P.86, POCKET MAP A14

Tımarcı Sok 3B, Galata ⓣ 0212 293 2055. Daily 9am–11pm.

This cosy café is well known for its superb fixed menu breakfast spread (₺40). Sit down to enjoy a mouthwatering array of dishes that include homemade organic jams, Georgian pancakes (the owner is of Georgian origin), several different cheeses, dressed olives and much more. One breakfast is generally enough for two people, and there are lots of other options for later in the day.

Fasuli

MAP P.86, POCKET MAP C14

İskele Cad 10–12 ⓣ 1 Tophane ⓣ 0212 243 6580. Mon–Fri 8am–11pm, Sat & Sun 9am–11pm.

White beans in tomato sauce (*kuru fasulye*) are a standard Turkish dish – here they are an art form. The tender, melt-in-your-mouth beans are grown in the foothills of the Pontic Alps, high above the owners' native Trabzon on the Black Sea, then smothered in a butter-rich tomato sauce. They make for a bargain (₺13) lunchtime treat, but there's much else to choose from besides. The restaurant, housed in an attractive period building, has a pleasant roof terrace. Unlicensed.

Galata Konak

MAP P.86, POCKET MAP A15

Haci Ali Sok 2 ⓣ 0212 252 5346, ⓦ www. galatakonak.com.tr. Daily 9am–midnight.

Really two places in one, the ground-floor patisserie is great for a range of quality Turkish and European-style cakes and desserts. Upstairs, reached by the antiquated lift original to this turn-of-the-nineteenth-century building, is a popular roof-terrace restaurant with a range of local and international dishes ranging from *menemen*, a scrambled egg, onion and pepper delight, to pasta dishes (₺14 and ₺23 and up respectively). It's especially packed for Sunday brunch. Great views but unlicensed.

Karaköy Güllüoğlu

MAP P.86, POCKET MAP B15

Rihtim Cad 17 ⓣ 0212 293 0910, ⓦ www.karakoylokantasi.com. Mon–Wed 7am–midnight, Thurs–Sat 7am–1am, Sun 8am–1am.

This cavernous place is certainly not the cheapest in the city for *baklava* and other Turkish nut and pastry concoctions, but it's arguably the best. It's invariably packed with locals tucking into walnut- or pistachio-rich *baklava*, which is rich and buttery with a dry texture (cheaper places often skimp on the nuts and overdo the syrup). Often, it comes with a splodge of chewy Maraş ice cream. Unlicensed.

Velvet Cafe

MAP P.86, POCKET MAP A15

Büyük Hendek Cad, Galata ⓣ 0507 867 3761. Tues–Sun 10am–8.30pm.

This eccentric, vintage café is a calm, quiet place to catch your breath at. One of the most endearing features is the coffee cups from all over the world, some of them are antiques – the pleasure of drinking from them is unforgettable. Try the delicious homemade desserts.

Restaurants

Galata House

MAP P.86, POCKET MAP A15
Galata Kulesi Sok 61 ☎ 0212 245 1861.
Tues–Sun 2pm–midnight, live music from 8pm.

Intimate, fifty-seater restaurant (booking advised) atmospherically housed in the old British Prison just down from the Galata Tower – ask owners Mete and Nadire to point out some of the graffiti left by former inmates and to give you a run-down of the whole history of this fascinating little quarter. Georgian-influenced cuisine is a real draw here – try the savoury stuffed dumplings. There's a nice garden out back, too. Mains ₺30 and up. Licensed.

Güney

MAP P.86, POCKET MAP A14
Kuledibi Sah Kapısı 6 ☎ 0212 249 0393.
Mon–Sat 7am–1.30pm.

Once a down to earth *lokanta*, today *Güney* serves a wide range of traditional Turkish and international dishes, from kebabs to pizzas, *pide* to steaks. Standards remain high, and the interior is stylish. The location, right on the square below the tower, is appealing and the food is good value with mains from ₺14. Licensed.

Karaköy Lokantası

MAP P.86, POCKET MAP C15
Kermankeş Cad 37/A ☎ 0212 292 4455.
Mon–Sat noon–4pm & 6pm–midnight, Sun 4pm–midnight.

Frequented by local office workers and merchants by day and a more sophisticated crowd by night, this is one of the most atmospheric places to eat in the city, with its beautiful turquoise-tiled interior

and excellent waterfront location. The service and food are top-notch, with a particularly enticing range of veggie and seafood starters, fish of the day mains and kebabs from ₺22. Licensed.

Nola Galata

MAP P.86, POCKET MAP A15
Galata Kulesi Sok 10 ☎ 0212 243 1717.
Mon–Thurs noon–midnight, Fri 11am–2am, Sat–Sun 11am–3am.

Though located in a historical area, this place is quite modern in ambience. Mains cost from ₺40, there are cold and hot *mezes*, and if the soup of the day (₺16) is chestnut – do not hesitate to order it. The restaurant also has a big, beautiful garden.

Bars

Ritim Galata

MAP P.86, POCKET MAP A15
Galata Kulesi Sok 3/C ☎ 0212 292 4929.
Mon–Sat 11am–4am, Sun 11am–midnight.

Between the Galata Tower and *Nardis Jazz Club*, this laidback little bar combines a stylish exposed brick and mezzanine-floor split interior with mellow sounds from the DJ and a decent Turkish and international menu. There are tables out on the cobbled street for hot evenings – and the smokers.

The Tower Pub

MAP P.86, POCKET MAP A15
Galata Kulesi Sok 4 ☎ 0212 243 7656,
🌐 thetowerpub.com. Daily 9am–midnight.

This is a Turkish take on an English pub complete with TV screens showing football and you can play darts. It's hospitable and laid back, a nice stop on a pub crawl or a good place to go to with friends. Whiskey shots between ₺28 and 58.

Unter

MAP P.86, POCKET MAP C15
Kara Ali Kaptan Sok 4 ☎ 0212 244 5151,

Ritim Galata

Ⓦ unter.com.tr. Tues–Fri noon–11.30pm, Sat 9am–2am, Sun 9am–8pm.
This is the cool, young Istanbulite's drinking den of choice in hip Karaköy. But there's more to *Unter* than mere alcohol, as it prides itself on a constantly changing menu of organic dishes, and things pick up on Thursday, Friday and Saturday nights, when assorted DJs take centre stage. Beers available from ₺20 (50cl), and cocktails from ₺38.

Clubs & venues

Fosil
MAP P.86, POCKET MAP B15
Kemeraltı Caddesi 16/A Ⓣ 0552 218 0762.
Fri noon–4pm & 6pm–4am, Sat 6pm–midnight.
Nowhere is more indicative of this once gritty neighbourhood's transformation from dockland grit to urban hip than this very cool bar and club, which has an interior decorated with exposed piping, bricks and bare bulbs. The narrow entrance way leaves you unprepared for the spectacular views across the Bosphorus once you're inside. It gets very busy on Friday and Saturday nights, despite beer prices ranging from ₺16–22, cocktails ₺30–50.

Nardis Jazz Club
MAP P.86, POCKET MAP A15
Kuledibi Sok 14 Ⓣ 0212 244 6327,
Ⓦ nardisjazz.com. Sets start Mon–Thurs 9.30pm, Fri & Sat 11.30pm. Admission ₺40–60.
This is one of the most accessible and intimate jazz clubs in the city, with the usual roster of (very talented) Turkish jazz performers complemented by a whole host of international artists. Admission prices are fairly reasonable, especially when you consider the location and that it attracts fans of all ages. You can expect an atmospheric bare-brick interior, as well as a bar-grub-type menu.

Beyoğlu and Taksim

Draped across the hilltop above Galata is Beyoğlu, the frenetic entertainment quarter of the metropolis. Heart of the action is one-and-a-half-kilometre-long İstiklal Caddesi (Independence Street), running from the upper Tünel station north to bland but impressively vast Taksim Square. From the seventeenth century onwards this became the European quarter of the city, home to the palatial residences of foreign merchants, ambassadors and members of the city's Greek and Armenian communities. Typically late nineteenth-century Neoclassical, Art Nouveau and Secessionist-style apartment blocks line the streets, punctuated by grand consular buildings, churches and period arcades. Beneath their grand facades, Istanbulites and foreign visitors shop, visit a gallery, take in a film, head up to a rooftop bar to watch the sun sink over the old city across the water and while away the night at a trendy club or live music venue.

Istanbul Modern

MAP P.96, POCKET MAP A13

The city's answer to London's Tate Modern might not be quite so large or cutting-edge but succeeds in bringing contemporary art to the heart of this thriving metropolis. First founded in 2004, the gallery has recently moved out of its landmark waterfront location and temporarily moved to the Union Française 19th century building designed by the French architect Alexandre Vallaury. The museum's permanent collection and temporary exhibits are spread over six floors. Due to lack of space the museum's functions are constrained and limited - but by no means any less vigorous. The photography collection is on the top floor, all the other permanent collections are exhibited in a selective fashion and on a changing schedule.

Upon the completion of the Galata Port project, Istanbul Modern will return to its original Karaköy location, albeit to a different, purpose built building which will be designed by Renzo Piano, an Italian Pritzker Prize winning architect whose fresh mind is, amongst others, behind the shape of the Shard (London). Although the project has not yet even been made public, the new Istanbul Modern is supposed to open in 2021.

İstiklal Caddesi: Tünel to Galatasaray Meydani

MAP P.96, POCKET MAP B13–D11

Leaving the upper İstiklal Tünel station and following the antique tramline round onto İstiklal Caddesi, the first sight of interest is the beautiful curvilinear Art Nouveau facade of the **Botter House**, built in 1901 by Italian architect D'Aronco for the Dutch tailor to Sultan Abdülhamit II. A little way beyond, best reached by heading down steep Kumbaracı Sokak, the pretty Anglican **Crimea Memorial Church** or Christ

Church was constructed in 1868 to commemorate those who fell in the Crimean War. The architect was G.E. Street, also responsible for the Royal Courts of Justice in London. It's attractively set in a green, walled compound, and visitors are requested to leave a ₺10 donation, but it's not always open – try a Sunday morning service. Further up on the right, steps lead down to **St Mary Draperis** (Mon & Wed–Sat 10am–noon, Tues & Sun 2–6pm; Mass Mon–Fri 8am, Sun 9am), a Catholic church designed by Semprini in 1904 on the site of a 1678 original.

On the opposite side of the street, the defunct **Patisserie Markiz**, still advertised by gold-leaf lettering on the glass, has a stunning fin-de-siècle interior with a pair of faïence tile wall panels, Le Printemps and L'Automne, imported from France. It's now a fast-food café. Just north of Markiz is a pretty nineteenth-century arcade, Cite de Syrie (see page 98). Opposite the arcade is the **Borusan Arts & Cultural Centre** (İstiklal Cad 213 ☎0212 336 3280, ⓦborusansanat.com), which is home to one of Turkey's leading private orchestras and an art gallery. Continuing up İstiklal on the right is the impressive Dutch consulate, the **Palais de**

Crimea Memorial Church

Hollande, built in Neoclassical style in 1858. On the same side further up the **Merkez Han**, owned by Koç University, houses the Research Centre for Anatolian Studies, which has regular free exhibitions of an archeological and historical nature. Back on the right, set back from the road, is the very attractive **St Anthoine** (daily 8am–7pm; Mass Sun 10am), a Franciscan church with a red-brick Neogothic facade, built

Getting to, and around, İstiklal Caddesi (Beyoğlu)

You can reach İstiklal Caddesi from the old city on the T1 tram to Karaköy and then either walk up the hill or take the Tünel funicular (see page 146) to the southern end of the street. Alternatively, with the opening of the Haliç Bridge in 2013, you can now also use the M2 metro to Şişhane or Taksim. For the north Taksim end, it's possible to ride the T1 tram to Kabataş, then the F1 funicular to Taksim Square. Wherever you start, explorations are best done on foot, though judicious use of the antique tram that runs the whole length of the street, stopping at points en route (see page 146), is fun. From the northern suburbs, you can use the M2 metro to Taksim at the north end of İstiklal Caddesi, or Şişhane at the south end. Unless otherwise stated, these will be the best ways to visit the sights and venues in this chapter.

Beyoğlu & Taksim

BARS

360	15
Arpa Bar	21
Arsen Lüpen	3
Büyük Londra Oteli	17
Çukurcuma 49	12
James Joyce Irish Pub	5
KV	23
Leb-i-Derya	22
Limonlu Bahçe	19
Pasific	20
Ritim Bar	9
Solera	18

CLUBS & VENUES

Çinaralti Club Taksim	8
Gizli Bahçe	7
Kiki	13
Klein	2
Love Dance Point	1
Mektup	4
Mini Müzikhol	16
Peyote	6
Pixie Underground	14
Roxy	11
Salon İKSV	24
Tek Yön	10

CAFÉS

Canım Ciğerim	18
Dürümzade	5
Falafel House	1
Hayvore	10
Kafe Ara	11
Mandabatmaz	13
Nizam Pide	7
Saray	9
Twins Coffee Roasters	4
Van Kahvaltı Evi	17

RESTAURANTS

Antiochia	22
ÇokÇok	12
Ficcin	14
Haci Abdullah Lokantasi	6
İmroz	3
Kenan Üsta Ocakbaşı	3
Meze by Lemon Tree	16
Mikla	15
Refik	19
Sofyalı	21
Yeni Lokanta	20
Zübeyir	2

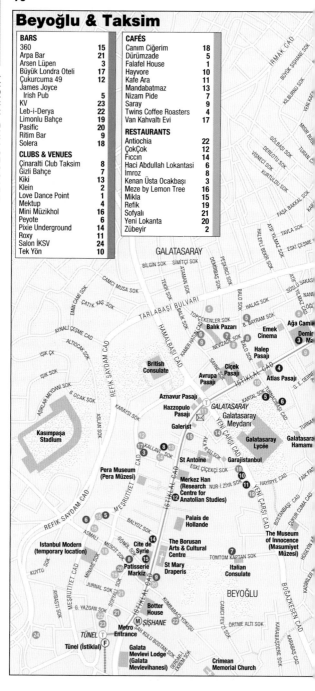

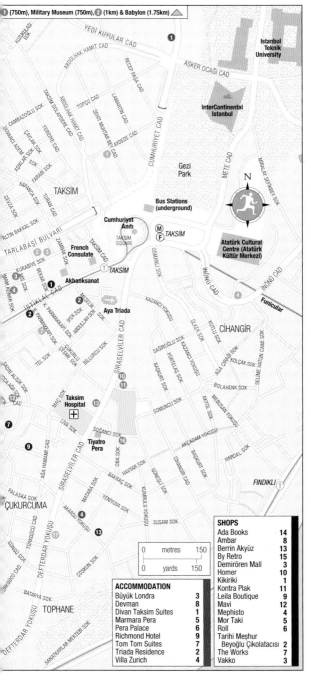

1 (750m), Military Museum (750m), 2 (1km) & Babylon (1.75km)

YEDİ KUYULAR CAD
ABDÜLHAK HAMİT CAD
RECEP PAŞA CAD
ASKER OCAĞI CAD
Istanbul Teknik University
TAKSIM DOLAPDERE CAD
ABDÜLHAK HAMİT CAD
TOPÇU CAD
ŞEHİT MUHTAR BEY CAD
LAMARTIN CAD
CUMHURIYET CAD
InterContinental Istanbul
CAMBAZOĞLU SOK
FERİDİYE CAD
METE CAD
ÇAYLAK SOK
DİVANCI ADEM SOK
Gezi Park
MİRALAY ŞEFİKBEY SOK
AŞIKLAR SOK
FARABİ SOK
TAKSİM
KAPANCA SOK
TURAN CAD
Bus Stations (underground)
CELZA SOK
Cumhuriyet Anıtı
TAKSİM SQUARE
M TAKSİM
F
ALTIN BAKKAL SOK
Atatürk Cultural Centre (Atatürk Kültür Merkezi)
TARLABAŞI BULVARI
ZAMBAK SOK
TAKSİM CAD
İNÖNÜ CAD
İNÖNÜ CAD
French Consulate
OSMANLI SOK
KURABİYE SOK
BEKAR SOK
T TAKSİM
Akbanksanat
Funicular
İMAM ADNAN SOK
ATİŞ SOK
İSTİKLAL CAD
KAZANCI YOKUŞU
K. PARMAKKAPI SOK
İPEK SOK
 H. SELİK
ÜLKER SOK
CİHANGİR
DEFNE SOK
Aya Triada
ABDÜLLAH SOK
KUTLU SOK
SAĞIRDLI SOK
AĞA ÇIRAĞI SOK
KOLÇAK SOK
SOK K. PARMAKKAPI SOK
ÇÜKÜRLÜ ÇEŞME SOK
BİLLURCU SOK
SİRASELVİLER CAD
PÜRTELAŞ SOK
KAZANCI YOKUŞU
SELİME HATUN CAMİİ SOK
TEL SOK
BAŞKURT SOK
AKYOL SOK
SADIH ALISIK SOK
MEŞRUSAN YOKUŞU
CA AĞA CAD
BOLAHENK SOK
Taksim Hospital
MAÇ SOK
SOMUNCU SOK
AKÇADAM YOKUŞU
LIVA SOK
BAŞKURT SOK
Tiyatro Pera
SOĞANCI SOK
OBA SOK
AĞA HAMAMI CAD
HAVYAR SOK
GÜNEŞLİ SOK
HARDAL SOK
CİHANGİR CAD
PALASKA SOK
SİRASELVİLER CAD
BAKRAÇ SOK
KUMBULU YOKUŞU
FINDIKLI T
ÇUKURCUMA
MATARA SOK
YENİYUVA SOK
SUSAM SOK
TÜRGÜCÜ CAD
AKARSU YOKUŞU
DEFTERDAR YOKUŞU
SÜNGÜ SOK
BATARYA SOK
TURNACIBAŞI CAD
ÇUKUR CUMA CAD
COŞKUN SOK
TOPHANE
DEFTERDAR YOKUŞU
SANATKARLAR MEKTEBİ SOK

N

| 0 | metres | 150 |
| 0 | yards | 150 |

SHOPS
Ada Books	14
Ambar	8
Berrin Akyüz	13
By Retro	15
Demirören Mall	3
Homer	10
Kikiriki	1
Kontra Plak	11
Leila Boutique	9
Mavi	12
Mephisto	4
Mor Taki	5
Roll	6
Tarihi Meşhur Beyoğlu Çikolatacısı	2
The Works	7
Vakko	3

ACCOMMODATION
Büyük Londra	3
Devman	8
Divan Taksim Suites	1
Marmara Pera	5
Pera Palace	6
Richmond Hotel	9
Tom Tom Suites	7
Triada Residence	2
Villa Zurich	4

in 1913 on the site of a much earlier church.

Meşrutiyet Caddesi

MAP P.96, POCKET MAP A13–B12

Running parallel to İstiklal Caddesi to the west and easily reached by cutting through one of the alleys joining them, this busy street is home to yet more fine turn-of-the-nineteenth-century buildings as well as a smattering of restaurants such as *Mikla* (see page 107), and the fin-de-siècle *Büyük Londra* hotel (see page 138) and its wonderful period bar (see page 108). At the north end of the street, where it joins Hamalbaşı Caddesi, is the grandiose, Renaissance-style **British Consulate**, built in 1855. Architect Charles Barry was also responsible for London's Houses of Parliament, but unfortunately today his work is semi-obscured by massive compound walls built after a terrorist bomb attack in 2003.

Pera Palace Hotel

MAP P.96, POCKET MAP A13

Meşrutiyet Cad 52 ⓘ 0212 377 4000, Ⓦ perapalace.com.

The most famous building on Meşrutiyet Caddesi, this grand hotel was completed in 1892 to accommodate gentry arriving in "Stamboul" on the trans-European Orient Express (see page 145). The architect was the prolific Frenchman Alexander Vallaury, also responsible for the Neoclassical Archeology Museum across in the old city (see page 42) and the Ottoman Bank down in Galata (see page 85). After years of neglect, it has been restored to its former glory, a necessary process that has resulted in a loss of some of its former character and a steep rise in prices but nostalgia buffs will be tempted to take afternoon tea and cake in the elegant ground-floor **tea rooms** and conjure up the shenanigans of past guests. These have included Greto Garbo and Zsa Zsa Gabor, Ernest Hemingway, Alfred Hitchcock and Atatürk, the founder of the

A passage to Europe

One of the delights of exploring İstiklal Caddesi and its offshoots is its nineteenth-century arcades. These attractive covered passages (*pasaj* in Turkish) are redolent of an era when Beyoğlu was Pera, İstiklal Caddesi the Grand Rue de Pera and the area home to a cosmopolitan mix of Armenians, Jews, Greeks and foreign residents. By far the best known and touristy is the **Cite de Pera**, more commonly known by its Turkish name **Çiçek Pasajı** (Flower Arcade), just north of Galatasaray Meydanı. Beautifully restored and today full of overpriced restaurants, its name derives from the White Russian émigrés who sold flowers here in the 1920s. The **Cite de Syrie** (**Suriye Pasajı** in Turkish), at the southern end of İstiklal Caddesi, was designed by a Greek architect in 1908 and has an ornate facade as well as housing the vintage clothing store *By Retro* (see page 102). Perhaps the most attractive of them all, however, is the **Passage d'Europe** (**Avrupa Pasajı**), which links Meşrutiyet Caddesi with Sahane Sok. Three storeys high, with a barrel-vaulted glazed roof and lined with Neoclassical statues, each of which represents a different craft, it's home today to some fine antique and souvenir shops. Other historic arcades include **Hazzopulo**, **Aznavur**, **Halep** (Aleppo) and **Atlas** pasajıs.

Nevizade Sokak

Turkish Republic (the room he regularly used, 401, is a museum). The notorious spy Mata Hari also stayed here and, last but not least, another regular, Agatha Christie, wrote *Murder on the Orient Express* in her favoured room, 411.

Pera Museum (Pera Müzesi)

MAP P.96, POCKET MAP A13
Meşrutiyet Cad 65 ☏ 0212 334 9900.
Tues–Sat 10am–7pm; Sun noon–6pm; Fri 6–10pm; free. ₺20.

As much an art gallery as a museum, the *Pera Museum* is housed in a beautifully restored late nineteenth-century building that was originally the prestigious *Bristol Hotel* – which was once a rival to the nearby *Pera Palace* and *Büyük Londra* hotels. On the first floor is a permanent exhibition of Kütahya tiles, similar to the more famous İznik ware, alongside a collection of surprisingly interesting weights and measures from across the ages. On the second floor are the works of Orientalist painters from the seventeenth to nineteenth centuries, the most striking (and valuable) of which is Osman

Hamdi's *Tortoise Trainer*, brought back to its native land from abroad for a cool $3.5 million in 2004. Floors three, four and five are devoted to temporary exhibitions – and frequently feature well-known artists. There's also a very decent café and shop for you to enjoy.

Nevizade Sokak

MAP P.96, POCKET MAP B11
This narrow pedestrian alley, running parallel to İstiklal Caddesi behind Çiçek Pasajı (see box opposite), is arguably the liveliest in the whole city. Lined by restaurants and bars, all with tables spilling out into the alleyway, it's worth fighting your way down just for the atmosphere or, even better, to join the raucous diners in a traditional *meyhane* (tavern) such as *İmroz* (see page 106).

Galatasaray Meydani

MAP P.96, POCKET MAP B12
This small square about halfway along İstiklal Caddesi is a stop for the antique tram. It's named after prestigious **Galatasaray Lycée** on the south side of the square, a school dating back to 1481,

Vintage furnitures at Çukurcuma

though the current building was erected in 1908. Students here formed one of Turkey's leading football clubs, Galatasaray, in 1905, and there's a small **museum** to the club (Tues–Sun 10am–7pm) in the restored Neoclassical building opposite. Hidden away below the square to the southeast is uber-cool **Garajistanbul** (Kaymakan Reşit Bey Sok 11, off Yeniçarşı Caddesi ☎0212 244 4499, ⓦgarajistanbul.org), which stands proudly as Istanbul's leading avant-garde performing arts and music venue.

Çukurcuma and Cihangir

MAP P.96, POCKET MAP C13 & E11

The warren of streets south and east of the northern section of İstiklal Caddesi make up the districts of Çukurcuma and Cihangir. The former is home to the fascinating Museum of Innocence and boasts a welter of bric-a-brac shops and vintage/alternative clothing outlets – especially on Turnacıbaşı Sokak. This steep, twisting street is also known for its famous Turkish baths, the **Galatasaray Hamamı** (Turnacı Başı Sok 24 ☎0212 249 4342, ⓦgalatasarayhamami.com; daily: men 7am–10pm, women 8.30am–8pm; bath only ₺80) which date back to 1481. Cihangir is the aspiring urban bohemian's

abode of choice in Istanbul, and has a number of trendy café-bars and hip shops.

The Museum of Innocence (Masumiyet Müzesi)

MAP P.96, POCKET MAP C13

Çukurcuma Cad 24 ☎0212 252 9738, ⓦmasumiyetmuzesi.org. Tues, Weds & Fri–Sun 10am–6pm; Thurs 10am–9pm ₺40; audio-guide ₺5.

It's probably only worth coming here if you've read the eponymous book by Turkey's Nobel Prize-winning author, Istanbulite Orhan Pamuk. In the book, the obsessive upper-class Kemal collects everyday items touched by his object of desire, an unsuitable young woman from an impoverished background. The objects are displayed as they were acquired, starting with over 4000 cigarette butts. The sequence finishes on the top floor with the bed where Kemal lays dying at the close of the novel.

İstiklal Caddesi: Galatasaray Meydan to Taksim

MAP P.96, POCKET MAP B12–D11

Although still lined by mainly grand nineteenth-century apartment blocks, İstiklal Caddesi becomes increasingly mainstream, period arcades apart (see page 98), as you approach Taksim Square. There are a number of **cinemas** here showing foreign films (see page 149) including the **Atlas** at İstiklal Cad 129 and further up on the left, the multiplex **Cinemaximum Fitaş** at no. 24–26. Also on the left is the Demirören shopping mall (see page 102) and, not far beyond it, the whitewashed **Ağa Camii** (1596), the only mosque on the street. A little way past the Fitaş cinema is the **Akbanksanat** (İstiklal Cad 8/A ☎0212 252 3500, ⓦakbanksanat. com), a culture and arts centre with exhibitions, a dance studio, theatre, cinema and café. Opposite is **Aya Triada**, a monumental Greek Orthodox church built in 1880.

Live music at Babylon

Istanbul's leading music venue (Birahane Sok 1; ☎ 0212 334 0190; ⓦ babylon.com.tr) has been living up to its "Babylon turns Istanbul on" motto for years – especially after its recent move out to a hip new venue, a refurbished former brewery in Bomonti. Acts include everything from world music bands to Turkish fusion. Get tickets for live music direct or via Biletix (ⓦ biletix.com).

Taksim Square (Taksim Meydani)

MAP P.96, POCKET MAP D10

Massive Taksim Square has little to recommend it bar its role as transport hub, but it has come to symbolize the secular identity of the Turkish Republic. It has long been a focal point for protests and in 2013 an occupy Wall Street type demonstration, protesting the destruction of a green area of the square, Gezi Park, brought Taksim to TV screens worldwide. Taksim Square takes its name from a reservoir built in 1732 (*taksim* means distribution) to distribute water through the city.

Military Museum (Asker Müzesi)

Valikonağı Cad, Harbiye Ⓜ **2 Osmanbey** ☎ **0212 233 2720. Wed–Sun 9am–4.30pm. ₺15.**

A fifteen-minute walk north of Taksim Square along busy Cumhüriyet Caddesi, this interesting museum traces the history of Turkish warfare and weaponry from the origins of the Turks in Central Asia through to the intervention of the Turkish Republic in Cyprus in 1974. Most exhibits are staidly displayed in dark-wood glass-fronted cabinets, but it's easy to while away an hour or two looking at everything from a huge section of the chain used to block the Golden Horn in the Byzantine era to heavy machine guns used in the Turkish defence of Gallipoli in 1915, and the embroidered tents used by campaigning sultans to a superb collection of Ottoman armour and weaponry. The **Mehter Band**, who accompanied the Ottoman war machine into battle from 1289 onwards, play rousing martial music on the first floor between 3 and 4pm each afternoon.

Asker Müzesi

Shops

Ada Books

MAP P.96, POCKET MAP B13

İstiklal Cad 20. ⓦ facebook.com/
istiklalada/. Mon–Fri 7am–10pm, Sat & Sun
9am–10pm.

Stocks a decent range of glossy
titles on Istanbul and Turkey along
with CDs, DVDs and magazines;
always busy because of its well-
regarded (licensed) café-restaurant.

Ambar

MAP P.96, POCKET MAP B12

Kallavi Sok 12, off İstiklal Cad. Mon–Sat
9am–7.30pm, Sun 12.30–7.30pm.

A family business concentrating on
organic and whole-foods as well as
natural soaps and lotions.

Berrin Akyüz

MAP P.97, POCKET MAP D13

Akarsu Yokuşu 22. Mon–Sat 10am–9pm.

Situated in trendy Cihangir, this
small boutique is a treasure-trove of
one-off fashion and home accessory
objects, from sheep-shaped
knitted bags to cushion covers, felt
jewellery and silk scarves.

By Retro

MAP P.96, POCKET MAP B13

Suriye Pasajı, off İstiklal Cad. Daily
10am–10pm.

A veritable cornucopia, hidden
away in the basement of this
historic arcade. Owner Hakan
trawls Europe for vintage and
retro clothing and decorative
household items such as old phones
and radios.

Demirören Mall

MAP P.96, POCKET MAP C11

İstiklal Cad. ⓦ facebook.com/
demirorenistiklal/. Daily 10am–10pm.

With so many high-street stores
and historic shopping passages it's
hard to see why İstiklal Caddesi
needed a mall, but if you're in
search of Gap, Mothercare or even
a Turkish fashion giant like Vakko
(see page 104) this accessible

location means you don't have to
head into the suburbs to find them.
Also houses a good cinema.

Homer

MAP P.96, POCKET MAP B12

Yeni Çarşı Cad 28. ⓦ facebook.com/
HomerKitabevi/. Mon–Sat 10am–7.30pm.

Great bookshop tucked away just
off İstiklal Caddesi with a superb
range of Turkey-related material
– art, archeology, literature and
politics as well as specialist books
on many other subjects – it even
has a good children's section.

Kikiriki

MAP P.97, POCKET MAP D11

İstiklal Cad 20. ☏ 0212 292 2323, ⓦ www.
kikiriki.com. Daily 10am–10pm.

An intriguing shop with bold and
exciting clothes that might not
appeal to all tastes. But if you're
looking for something unusual
and striking, this is the place to
go. Even the creative display is not
something you'd see in a usual
vintage shop.

Kontra Plak

MAP P.96, POCKET MAP B12

Kontra Plak Yeni Çarşı Cad 60/A,
Galatasaray. ☏ 0212 243 8680,
ⓦ kontrarecords.com. Daily 11am–9pm.

This hip basement record store
caters to cool young Istanbulites
and the youthful ex-pats who have
made this neighbourhood their
own. Browse through an impressive
range of records and CDs of all
genres, from Turkey and beyond.

Leila Boutique

MAP P.96, POCKET MAP C12

Altıpatlar Sok 6. ⓦ leilaconceptstore.com.
Mon–Fri 11am–8pm, Sat noon–8pm.

Leila Boutique has amassed a fine
collection of vintage clothes – from
the nineteenth century to the
1960s – as well as cushion-covers,
throws and the like.

Mavi

MAP P.96, POCKET MAP B12

İstiklal Cad 189/A. Mon–Sat 10am–10pm,

Mavi

Sun 10am–midnight.
Mavi is well known in Turkey for its quality denim goods and other clothing, and if you're after a non-crass souvenir T-shirt its ever-changing and witty range of Istanbul-inspired designs is worth checking out.

Mephisto

MAP P.96, POCKET MAP C11
İstiklal Cad 125, Beyoğlu. ☏ 0212 249 0696, ✆ mephisto.com.tr. Mon–Thurs 9am–midnight, Fri 9am–5pm, Sat 9am–1am, Sun 9am–11pm.
This modern book and music store stocks a good range of Turkish music CDs and is popular with young Istanbulites who head to its pleasant café to escape the throngs on the main shopping street outside.

Mor Taki

MAP P.96, POCKET MAP C12
Turnacıbaşı Sok 10B, off İstiklal Cad. Mon–Sat 10am–7.30pm.
At the İstiklal Caddesi end of this trendy street this chic, hole-in-the-wall outlet is worth a look for its range of alternative, handmade jewellery.

Roll

MAP P.96, POCKET MAP C12
Turnacıbaşı 38/1, off İstiklal Cad. Mon–Sat 10am–10pm, Sun noon–9.30pm.
In a grubby passage full of grungy alternative clothes stalls, this one stands out for its funny line of T-shirts inspired by Turkey's recent past, from iconic Turkish film characters to the logos of so-bad-they're-good Turkish cars.

Tarihi Meşhur Beyoğlu Çikolatacısı

MAP P.97, POCKET MAP C11
İstiklal Cad 69/A. Daily 11am–11pm.
Istanbulites love their *baklava* and traditional desserts, but they also have a passion for chocolate. Buy almond, hazelnut or pistachio slabs of the stuff from this chocolatier.

The Works

MAP P.97, POCKET MAP C12
Faik Paşa Sok 6. Mon–Sat 11am–6pm.
A muddle of retro delights awaits the visitor here, from tin toys to vintage Pepsi bottles and the chrome hood mascots of 1950s American cars. It supplied the nearby Museum of Innocence (see page 100) with some exhibits.

Kafe Ara

Vakko

MAP P.96, POCKET MAP C11
Demirören Mall, İstiklal Cad. Daily
10am–10pm.
For a Turkish take on mainstream
fashion for both men and women,
Vakko is a reliable choice – the fact
it's been in business over fifty years
speaks volumes about its quality
materials and timeless designs.

Cafés

Canım Ciğerim

MAP P.96, POCKET MAP A13
Minare Sok 1 ☎ 0212 252 6060, ⊛ www.
canimcigerim.com. Daily noon–midnight.
Just off lively Asmalımescit, "My
Dearest Liver" specializes in skewers
of small cubes of the tenderest liver
imaginable, dished up with salad
and fresh flatbread (₺26). Non-
offal-eaters may prefer the chicken
or lamb options. Unlicensed.

Dürümzade

MAP P.96, POCKET MAP B11
Kamer Hatun Cad 26/A ☎ 0212 249 0147.
Daily 8am–4am.
If you want to sit and linger, forget
this place. If you want to try a

dürüm (wrap) filled with the most
succulent chargrilled meat for a
bargain ₺8, then *Dürümzade* is for
you. One of the secrets employed
here is to get the very best, slightly
chewy flatbread, rub it with a
subtle blend of spices and toast
it on the grill before adding the
meat filling.

Falafel House

MAP P.97, POCKET MAP D10
Şehit Muhtar Cad 19, off Taksim Square
☎ 0212 253 7730. Daily 9am–1am.
Many Turkey first-timers assume
Middle Eastern street food like
hummus and falafel will be staples
here too – they're not. That's why
this cheap and cheerful Palestinian-
run place is such a great find. The
decor is greasy spoon, but there are
a few tables out on the street for
people-watching. Set-menu meals
from ₺20. Unlicensed.

Hayvore

MAP P.96, POCKET MAP C12
Turnacıbaşı Sok 4, off İstiklal Cad ☎ 0212
245 7501. Daily 7.30am–11.30pm.
Pick from a wide range of
steamtray dishes in this authentic,
eastern Black Sea restaurant –
there's the inevitable corn bread to
mop up the juices from delectable
chickpea or white bean stews (₺8),
or to accompany the excellent
cabbage soup. Unlicensed.

Kafe Ara

MAP P.96, POCKET MAP B12
Tosbağı Sok 8/A, off Yeniçarşı Cad ☎ 0212
245 4105. Mon–Fri 9am–11.30pm, Sat &
Sun 10am–11.30pm.
Owned by Turkey's leading
photographer, Armenian-
Istanbulite Ara Güler, this
sophisticated café is adorned with
marvellous black and white images
of his city. Mix of Turkish and
international dishes. Unlicensed.

Mandabatmaz

MAP P.96, POCKET MAP B12
Olivia Geçidi, off İstiklal Cad. ☎ 0212 243
7737. Daily 9am–11pm.

Having been superseded by tea as the national drink, Turkish coffee is not always as great as it would like to be. This tiny coffee joint is an exception. For just ₺5 you can sip a rich, velvet brew as good as you'll find anywhere in the Middle East. It's been going since 1967 but has remained resolutely unchanged since, with customers sitting on low stools in the cramped interior or out in the alley.

Nizam Pide

MAP P.97, POCKET MAP C11

Büyükparmakkapı Sok 18, off İstiklal Cad ☎ 0212 249 7918, ⓦ www.nizampide.com. Mon–Sat 8am–5am, Sun 9am–4am.

Pide is often described as Turkish pizza. It's actually rather different – essentially a large, oval semi-leavened flatbread baked in a wood oven with a variety of toppings – standards are cheddar-like *kaşarlı* cheese, chopped-meat *kuşbaşı* or *beyaz peynirli* – goat's cheese and parsley. This is a great place to try it. ₺15 and up. Unlicensed.

Saray

MAP P.96, POCKET MAP C11

İstiklal Cad 107 ☎ 0212 292 3434. Daily 6am–4am.

This popular place, spread over several floors, does main meals but is best known for its splendid traditional desserts, from *tavuk göğüsü* (a milk pudding enhanced with semolina and chicken breast) to *fırın sutlaç* (oven-baked rice pudding). Unlicensed.

Twins Coffee Roasters

MAP P.97, POCKET MAP E10

İnönü Cad 23 ☎ 0532 738 9601.Mon–Fri 7.30am–8pm, Sat & Sun 10am–8pm.

A very pleasant breakfast option, with a few but good choices for a morning or midday snack, just right to give you some more energy to keep walking around the city. The coffee is recommended and the atmosphere is pleasant.

Van Kahvaltı Evi

MAP P.97, POCKET MAP D13

Van Kahvaltı Evi Defterdar Yokuşu 52/A, Cihangir ☎ 0212 293 6437. Daily 8am–5pm.

This all-day breakfast place brings the cuisine of far-flung Van, a predominantly Kurdish city in eastern Turkey, to Istanbul. As well as Turkish standards like olives and cheeses, you can try *kavut* (roasted wheat flour blended with honey and walnuts), *jajı* (yoghurt and cottage cheese) and clotted cream with honey. Full breakfasts from ₺20. Extremely busy weekend mornings/lunchtimes.

Restaurants

Antiochia

MAP P.96, POCKET MAP A13

General Yazgan Sok 3, Asmalımescit ☎ 0212 244 0820, ⓦ www.antiochiaconcept.com. Mon–Sat noon–midnight.

Owner Lale Balcı has written about the unique cuisine of her native Hatay, close to the Syrian border, and she and her chefs certainly know how to prepare it. Kebabs (from ₺35) done Hatay-style are

Hacı Abdullah Lokantası

Kenan Usta Ocakbaşı

juicier and spicier than the standard issue but the real pull is the tasty *meze*, including the thyme salad *zahter* and spicy hot *muammara*, a walnut and hot pepper dip. Licensed.

ÇokÇok

MAP P.96, POCKET MAP B12
Meşrutiyet Cad 51 ⓣ 0212 292 6496, Ⓦ www.cokcok.com.tr. Mon 6pm–midnight, Tues–Sun noon–midnight.

If you can't survive Istanbul without a Thai fix, this is a worthy option, with a Thai chef, the freshest ingredients and stylish surroundings. Best option is the lunchtime special, but the good choice of cocktails is a bonus for a "night-out" feast. Mains from ₺28.

Ficcin

MAP P.96, POCKET MAP B12
Kallavi Sok 13, off İstiklal Cad ⓣ 0212 293 3786. Tues–Sat 8am–midnight.

Not the most sophisticated place in Beyoğlu but nicely located down a quiet alley with street tables and great value for Caucasus-style dishes such as the eponymous *ficcin*, a tasty meat pie, rocket

soup and the yoghurt-drenched Caucasian ravioli *Çerkez mantısı*. Mains from ₺16. Licensed.

Haci Abdullah Lokantasi

MAP P.96, POCKET MAP C11
Sakızağacı Cad 17, off İstiklal Cad ⓣ 0212 245 7501, Ⓦ haciabdullah.com.tr. Daily 9am–11pm.

A Beyoğlu institution that's been serving traditional Turkish fare (soups, steamtray dishes, grills, pies and desserts) since 1888. It's right by the Ağa Camii (see page 100) so there's no alcohol, and it does trade on its reputation, so it's not the cheapest; but the food is good and the period ambience suitably sedate. Mains ₺22–65.

İmroz

MAP P.96, POCKET MAP B11
Nevizade Sok 24, off İstiklal Cad ⓣ 0212 249 9073. Daily noon–1am.

This perennially popular *meyhane* has been in business since 1941, and makes the perfect choice for a memorable *rakı* and fish-fuelled night out – eat, drink, talk (if you can make yourself heard over the other diners) and relax as you watch the almost constant procession of revellers parading by. Mains here start from ₺18.

Kenan Üsta Ocakbaşı

MAP P.97, POCKET MAP D11
Kurabiye Sok 18, off İstiklal Cad ☏ 0212 293 5611. Daily 11am–1am.

This place is a real treat for all carnivores, as the master-chef here has been grilling choice cuts of meat over charcoal for over forty years. The *meze* are all freshly prepared to order, and the kebabs (from ₺30) and other meat are served up with piles of thin, unleavened bread (*lavaş*), deftly wiped across the grill and smeared with oil and spices. There are tables out on the street if you'd rather dine outside, and it's licensed.

Meze by Lemon Tree

MAP P.96, POCKET MAP A13
Meşrutiyet Cad 83/B ☏ 0212 252 8203, ⓦ mezze.com.tr. Daily 6pm–11.30pm.

This is an innovative and stylish place near the *Pera Palace Hotel*, and unsurprisingly given its name, *meze* are the real highlight here. What's on offer changes according to the seasons, just like the rest of the menu. Choose one of the meat or fish mains, which start at ₺32, or indulge in the two-person taster menu for ₺196, which includes a great choice of hot and cold *meze*, a main and dessert. Licensed.

Mikla

MAP P.96, POCKET MAP A13
Marmara Pera Hotel, Meşrutiyet Cad 167/185 ☏ 0212 293 5656, ⓦ www. miklarestaurant.com. Mon–Sat 6pm–2am.

Seventeen floors up on the roof of the towering *Marmara Pera Hotel* (see page 138) this restaurant has sensational views over the old city and Bosphorus as well as excellent food – Turkish/Mediterranean with a Scandinavian twist. The fixed menu is ₺185 and there's wine by the glass from ₺25. It's expensive but worth it for the ambience and views – dress up a bit for this one.

Refik

MAP P.96, POCKET MAP A13
Sofyalı Sok 10–12, off İstiklal Cad ☏ 0212 245 7879, ⓦ facebook.com/ refikrestaurant/. Mon–Sat noon–midnight, Sun noon–1am.

A low-key place in a busy alley, this intellectual take on the *meyhane* has a good range of *meze* – including some Black Sea specialities – and the usual grilled fish and meat mains. The set menu is good value if you're in the drinking mood as all local drinks are included in the price.

Sofyalı

MAP P.96, POCKET MAP A13
Sofyalı Sok 9, off İstiklal Cad ☏ 0212 252 3810, ⓦ www.sofyali.com.tr. Mon–Sat 2pm–1am.

A sophisticated *meyhane* with a soothing interior, all white walls, stripped wood floors and antique furniture, this busy place is in heavy demand so best to book ahead – especially for Friday and Saturday evenings and for the outside tables. The *meze* are particularly good, with meat mains and fish on request. Also has a good range of wines and *rakı*.

Yeni Lokanta

MAP P.96, POCKET MAP B13
Kumbaracı Yokuşu 66 ☏ 0212 292 2550, ⓦ www.yenilokanta.com. Mon–Sat noon–1am.

Owner/chef Çivan Er was the innovative cook at the famous *Changa* restaurant before opening his own place at the head of this steep alley. Here he concentrates on traditional Anatolian and southeastern Turkish favourites, but gives them a few novel tweaks. For a restaurant that brings droves of well-heeled Istanbulites in from wealthy suburbs, it's reasonably priced (mains ₺45 and up), and both the cocktail and wine lists are sound. Advance reservation essential.

Zübeyir

MAP P.97, POCKET MAP C11
Bekar Sok 28 ☎ 0212 293 3951,
ⓦ zubeyirocakbasi.com.tr. Daily noon–midnight.

This little place is located at the heart of the Beyoğlu district. Choose a seat around the open charcoal grill and watch your food being made – very pleasant when it's cold, slightly less so when it's the middle of summer.

Bars

360

MAP P.96, POCKET MAP B12
Mısır Apartmanı 311, İstiklal Cad ☎ 0212 251 1042. Sun–Thurs noon–2am, Fri & Sat noon–4am.

The top floor of this fine nineteenth-century apartment block is home to this upmarket bar-restaurant. Take the lift and – if suitably attired – you can enjoy the 360° views and sip a drink whose price reflects the grandeur of the vista.

Arpa Bar

MAP P.96, POCKET MAP A13
General Yazgan Sok 5 ☎ 0212 249 0550. Daily 9am–2pm.

This small, corner-plot bar has a very pleasant bare-brick interior, jazz soundtrack and beers priced between ₺11–16. It's a good choice for a quiet drink in bustling Asmalımescit.

Arsen Lüpen

MAP P.96, POCKET MAP C11
Mis Sok 15 ☎ 0532 676 3943. Daily 1pm–5am.

A two-floor rustic bar with a dance floor on the bottom floor and a terrace with a wonderful view upstairs. On weekends they play live music – folk, jazz, rock and one day a week there is a Spoken Word night when artists read out their latest pieces or sing their own songs (travelling writers are welcome, too). The bar is a little hard to find, so you might need to ask around.

Büyük Londra Oteli

MAP P.96, POCKET MAP B12
Meşrutiyet Cad 117 ☎ 0212 245 0670. Daily noon–11pm.

The bar of this hotel (see page 138), little changed since it first opened in the late nineteenth century to serve drinks to guests arriving on the *Orient Express*, is all dark wood, gilt and antique furnishings – there's even a parrot in a suitably ornate cage. Take the antiquated lift up to the fine roof bar in warm weather.

Çukurcuma 49

MAP P.96, POCKET MAP C12
Turnacıbaşı Sok 49/A ☎ 0212 249 0048, Sun–Thurs 9.30am–11pm, Fri & Sat 9am–1am.

This split-level bar-cum-pizzeria based in a former office building is a suitably fashionable hangout for the trendy neighbourhood of Çukurcuma. Exposed brick walls and lots of natural materials give it the homely atmosphere that attracts locals and the district's expat community in equal numbers – that, and the good-value wines from the Aegean Turkish island of Bozcaada (from ₺17.5).

James Joyce Irish Pub

MAP P.96, POCKET MAP B11
Irish Centre, Balo Sok 26 ☎ 0212 244 7973, ⓦ facebook.com/irishpubthejamesjoyce. Sun–Thurs 12.30pm–2am, Fri & Sat 12.30pm–4am.

Situated in one of the very liveliest parts of Beyoğlu, this rambling place gets packed to bursting point for big-screen sports events and when there's a band on (most evenings). Guinness is ₺18 for 50cl, and there's a wide range of continental lagers, as well as local beers for ₺12.

KV

MAP P.96, POCKET MAP A13
Tünel Gecidi 6, off İstiklal Cad ☎ 0212 251 4338. Daily 8.30am–2am.

Sophisticated place at the Asmalımescit entrance to the very pretty nineteenth-century Tünel passage, good in summer when you can sit at outside tables in the potted plant-lined passageway and enjoy a decent glass of wine and a light meal.

Leb-i-Derya

MAP P.96, POCKET MAP B13
Kumbaracı Yokuşu 57/6 ☎ 0541 366 8480, ⓦ www.lebiderya.com. Daily 4pm–2am.
It's not cheap, but this is one of Beyoğlu's best upmarket bars, attracting a well-off but not particularly posey crowd. The lounge has a great picture window with stunning views down to the confluence of the Golden Horn with the Bosphorus, and there's a small roof terrace for warm evenings. Decent cocktails and a (pricey) international-style food menu.

Limonlu Bahçe

MAP P.96, POCKET MAP B12
Yeniçarşı Cad 74 ☎ 0212 252 1094, ⓦ limonlubahcebeyoglu.com. Daily 10am–2am.
A short stroll downhill from bustling İstiklal Caddesi, this is worth seeking out for its quiet garden, bar grub and decently priced beers and cocktails (beers from ₺14, wine by the glass from ₺24).

Pasific

MAP P.96, POCKET MAP B13
Sofyalı Sok 4, off Asmalımescit ☎ 0212 292 7642. Daily noon–3am.
Cheap bar on a narrow, busy alley, a good bet for an early beer or two, though they also draw in punters with cheap shot deals. The soundtrack is generally rock, the vibe studenty, the flat-screen TV permanently tuned to Akıllı TV – a channel devoted to amusing mishaps from around the world.

Ritim Bar

MAP P.96, POCKET MAP B11
Sahane Sok 20, Balık Pazarı ☎ 0539 859 0095. Daily 10am–5pm.
No-frills bar attracting a mix of locals and visitors – the owner also runs the popular *World House Hostel* (see page 138) – with reasonably priced drinks. Really gets going on summer weekends when the party-minded pack the rooftop to dance to a mix of favourite dance sounds.

Büyük Londra Oteli

Solera

MAP P.96, POCKET MAP B12
Yeniçarşı Cad 44, Galatasaray ☎ 0212 252
2719, ⓦ facebook.com/solerawinery/. Daily
11am–2am.

Wine bars are few and far between
in Istanbul, so to come across this
one serving over 1000 Turkish
and international wines is a near
miracle – especially when the
prices are reasonable too (₺12 per
glass, bottles ₺44 and up). The
wine is best enjoyed with one
of owner Suleyman Er's *meze*
sampler plates.

Clubs & venues

Çinaralti Club Taksim

MAP P.96, POCKET MAP B11
Balo Sok 14 ☎ 0542 721 8090. Daily
9pm–7.30am.

A two-floor club with a pleasant
atmosphere and good music.

Gizli Bahçe

MAP P.97, POCKET MAP B11
Nevizade Sok 27 ☎ 0212 249 2192. Daily
hours vary.

This upstairs club provides a
chilled contrast to the mayhem
of Nevizade Sokak (see page
99) below. Lounge on sofas
or watch the action below
from a balcony listening to an
eclectic mix of dance, soul, blues
and jazz.

Kiki

Kiki

MAP P.97, POCKET MAP D12
Siraselviler Cad 42. ☎ 0212 243 5373,
ⓦ kiki.com.tr. Tues–Sat 6pm–4am.

There's no Bosphorus bling down
at understated *Kiki*, a cool club that
attracts a younger crowd who go
for the deep house DJs. The club
is spread over three floors and is
best in summer on the roof terrace.
Drinks are pricey at ₺8 for a small
beer, but entry is free.

Klein

MAP P.97, POCKET MAP D10
Harbiye Cumhüriyet Cad 4 ☎ 0212 291
8440. Fri & Sat 11pm–4am.

Slightly inconveniently located a
kilometre north of Taksim Square,
this is the subterranean venue of
choice for young, stylish and largely
black-clad Istanbul youths seeking
like-minded souls, electronica and
trendy drinks served from two long
bars.

Love Dance Point

MAP P.97, POCKET MAP D10
Cumhüriyet Cad 349 Ⓜ 2 Osmanbey
☎ 0212 232 5683, ⓦ www.lovedp.net.
Fri–Sat 11.30pm–5am.

Long-running gay club in this
prosperous suburb north of Taksim
Square, opposite the Military
Museum (see page 101), it makes
a gentle introduction to the city's
gay scene. The music is pop/dance,
both domestic and international.

Mektup

MAP P.96, POCKET MAP C11
İmam Adnan Sok 20, off İstiklal Cad
☎ 0212 251 0740, ⓦ mektupbar.com. Daily
noon–4am.

Even young, hip Istanbulites have
great respect for traditional Turkish
music, and *Mektup* offers this
(Türkü) to a very high standard – it
has seen sets by notable artists such
as Ebru Destan and Tuğbay Özay.
Booking is advisable, especially
at weekends.

Mini Müzikhol

MAP P.97, POCKET MAP D12
Soğancı Sok 7, off Sıraselvıler Cad ☎ 0212
245 1996, ⓦ minimuzikhol.com. Wed–Sat
10pm–5.30am.

The artfully contrived interior and
urbane clientele make this one of
the best music venues if you're into
sophisticated dance and electronica,
especially as it attracts a regular
supply of well-known international
(and local) DJs.

Peyote

MAP P.96, POCKET MAP B11
Kameriye Sok 4 ☎ 0212 251 4398,
ⓦ peyote.com.tr. Daily 3pm–4am.

This is the best place in the city for
alternative music, with electronica
on the first floor, live bands on
the second and an attractive roof
terrace where a mixed bag of
musical genres are spun.

Pixie Underground

MAP P.96, POCKET MAP B12
Toşbaşağa Sok 12, off İstiklal Cad. Fri &
Sat 6pm–4am.

Istanbul's only bass music
club, this is the place to head
for dubstep, drum'n'bass and
jungle. Istanbul's up-and-coming
producers cut their teeth in this
welcoming place, and entry is free
most nights, with a nominal sum
on bigger occasions.

Roxy

MAP P.96, POCKET MAP D12
Aslanyatağı Sok 1/3 ☎ 0212 249 1283,
ⓦ roxy.com.tr. Fri & Sat 10pm–5am.

Pixie Underground

Well-established club a little off
the main Beyoğlu circuit, *Roxy*
mixes contemporary Turkish music
and live acts with foreign singers
and bands (Marc Almond and
Ben Harper have played here).
Electronica, rock, blues and world
music all feature, playing to a well-
heeled Istanbulite crowd.

Salon İKSV

MAP P.96, POCKET MAP A14
Sadi Konuralp Cad 5 ☎ 0212 3340755,
ⓦ saloniksv.com. Opening hours vary.

With funding from Istanbul
Foundation for Culture and Arts
(İKSV), this slightly out of the way
venue hosts a variety of acts, from
rock, jazz and world music concerts
– many reasonably well-known
internationally – to contemporary
dance and classical music. Tickets in
advance from Biletix (ⓦ biletix.com).

Tek Yön

MAP P.96, POCKET MAP D12
Siraselviler Cad 63 ☎ 0212 233 0654. Daily
11pm–5am.

Down canyon-like Siraselviler
Caddesi and best approached from
the southeast corner of Taksim
Square, this popular "mainstream"
gay venue has a large dancefloor,
a big garden out back and regular
drag-shows – inevitably, it gets
packed solid on Friday and
Saturday evenings.

Beşiktaş and Ortaköy

The waterfront Dolmabahçe Palace, a grandiose European-style residence for the Ottoman Empire's last sultans, is the major tourist attraction this side of the Golden Horn. Northeast along the Bosphorus-front is Beşiktaş. Home to the most working class of the city's "big three" football teams, it's rapidly emerging from a cocoon of urban decay and possesses a youthful vibrancy thanks to its huge student population. Further along is Yıldız Park, a vast, wooded park dotted with imperial pavilions. Beyond it, Ortaköy retains some feel of the fishing village it once was. It has a lovely Baroque-style mosque and a lively waterfront lined with posh cafés. Just to the northeast, virtually underneath the continent-spanning Bosphorus Bridge, a handful of glitzy Bosphorus-front clubs play host to the city's glamorous elite and visiting celebrities.

Dolmabahçe Palace (Dolmabahçe Sarayı)

MAP P.114
Dolmabahçe Cad 🚊 1 Kabataş, buses #25/E, #28 ☎ 0212 236 9000, 🖥 www. millisaraylar.gov.tr/ziyaret-bilgileri. Tues–Sun 9am–4pm. Selamlık ₺60, harem ₺40.
The apogee of imperial excess and home to the last sultans of the ailing Ottoman Empire after the imperial retinue moved here from Topkapı in 1853, the palace was completed in 1856. Its decidedly European appearance, influenced by the Baroque, Neoclassical and Rococo styles, makes it more akin to Versailles than a traditional Muslim palace – although it was divided, according to Islamic precepts, into an area for men only (selamlık) and women only (harem) as well as administrative quarters. Taking up a whopping 600m of Bosphorus waterfront, the palace's ornate, marble frontage is arguably best viewed from a Bosphorus cruise (see page 126). This grandiose building was primarily the work of two leading Armenian Istanbul architects, Karabet Balian and his son Nikoğos, though the showy interior, gilded with some fourteen tonnes of gold leaf, was masterminded by French decorator Sechan. The palace can only be visited as part of a guided tour, meaning visitors, usually in maximum groups of fifty, are herded through at a brisk pace. Of most interest are the hamam, complete with an incongruously luxurious squat toilet, the marquetry-work masterpiece that is the dining hall parquet floor and, in the ceremonial hall, suspended from a ceiling double the height of the other rooms, a magnificently over the top Bohemian crystal chandelier weighing 4.5 tonnes and glowing with 750 lamps, a suitably flamboyant gift from Queen Victoria.

Palace Collections Museum (Saray Koleksiyonları Müzesi)

MAP P.114
Dolmabahçe Cad 🚊 1 Kabataş, buses #25/E, #28 ☎ 0212 236 9000. Tues–Sun 9am–5pm. ₺20.

If you've balked at the steep admission price to the palace, it's worth checking out this unusual museum, which will give you a fascinating and more down-to-earth insight into how the opulent residence functioned. For here, displayed in what were the former kitchens of Dolmabahçe, are over all taken from the palace. They range from those you might expect, like Limoges porcelain tea services and the mother-of-pearl-inlaid wooden clogs used in the hamam, through to Singer sewing machines and, dating from the period when Atatürk was resident here, a 1930s Ericcson switchboard so crucial in a labyrinthine complex of over four hundred rooms. The kitchens themselves have been nicely restored too – needless to say, there's no gilt in sight here.

Naval Museum (Deniz Müzesi)

MAP P.114
Barbaros Meydanı ⊕ 1 Kabataş, buses

#25/E, #28, #40, #40/T, #42/T ☎ 0212 327 4346, ⓦ denizmuzeleri.tsk.tr. Tues–Fri 9am–5pm, Sat & Sun 10am–6pm. ₺8.5; audio-guide ₺21.

Housed in a state-of-the-art new building completed in 2013, this fine museum, with huge windows overlooking the Bosphorus, has over 20,000m of exhibition space. At the heart of the museum is a superb collection of restored caïques, elegant boats once used to row the sultans to and from their homes along the Bosphorus. The largest of these caïques, dating from 1648, needed some 144 oarsmen to propel it. Downstairs is an exhibition devoted to woodcarving in the Ottoman navy, featuring some beautiful figureheads. There's also a café and kids' play area.

Çırağan Palace (Çırağan Sarayı)

MAP P.114
Çırağan Cad ⊕ 1 Kabataş, buses #25/E, #28, #40, #40/T, #42/T.

Guard at Dolmabahçe Sarayı

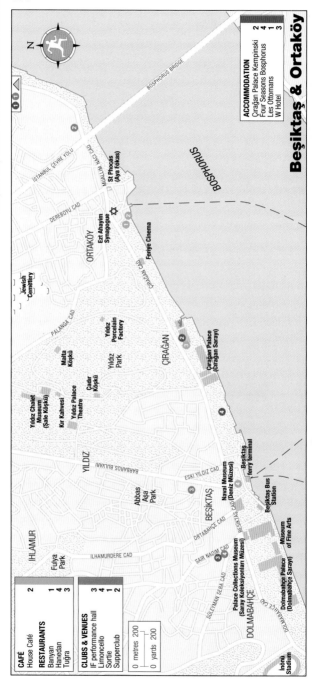

Beşiktaş & Ortaköy

BOSPHORUS BRIDGE

BOSPHORUS

ISTANBUL ÇEVRE YOLU

DEREBOYU CAD

MUALLIM NACI CAD

St Phocas
(Aya Fokas)

Ezt Ahayim
Synagogue

ORTAKÖY

Ferige Cinema

ÇIRAĞAN CAD

Jewish
Cemetery

PALANGA CAD

Yıldız
Porcelain
Factory

Malta
Köşkü

Yıldız
Park

Çadır
Köşkü

ÇIRAĞAN

Çırağan Palace
(Çırağan Sarayı)

Yıldız Chalet
Museum
(Şale Köşkü)

Kır Kahvesi

Yıldız Palace
Theatre

BARBAROS BULVARI

YILDIZ

ESKI YILDIZ CAD

Beşiktaş
ferry terminal

IHLAMUR

Fulya
Park

Abbas
Ağa
Park

Naval Museum
(Deniz Müzesi)

BEŞIKTAŞ

ORTABAHÇE CAD

BEŞIKTAŞ CAD

Beşiktaş Bus
Station

Museum
of Fine Arts

ILHAMURDERE CAD

ŞAIR NADIM CAD

SÜLEYMAN SEBA CAD

Palace Collections Museum
(Saray Koleksiyonları Müzesi)

DOLMABAHÇE

Dolmabahçe Palace
(Dolmabahçe Sarayı)

DOLMABAHÇE CAD

İnönü
Stadium

N

0 metres 200
0 yards   200

Today the luxurious *Çırağan Palace Kempinski* (see page 139), this imperial residence was originally constructed in 1855 for Sultan Abdülmecit, and is very much a mini-Dolmabahçe. What you see now, however, is much more recent, as the place burned down in 1910 and was derelict until its 1990 restoration and conversion to a hotel.

Yıldız Park

MAP P.114
Çırağan Cad ● 1 Kabataş, buses #25/E, #28, #40, #40/T, #42/T.

Sprawling down a steep hillside to busy Çırağan Caddesi and the Bosphorus beyond, this oasis of green, usually entered from the south gates opposite the Çırağan Palace, was the palace complex of Abdülhamit II for thirty years. The notoriously paranoid sultan moved here from the Dolmabahçe Palace as he feared the latter was too exposed to naval attacks. Today, it's a place to escape the city hustle and/or visit the pavilions of the palace, which were designed by the famous Italian architect D'Aronco. The main points of interest are located a ten- to fifteen-minute walk uphill from the park entrance on Çırağan Caddesi. The most visited is the **Yıldız Chalet Museum** (Şale Köşkü; Tues–Sun 9am–5pm; ₺20), an attractive, Swiss chalet-style pavilion dominated by the ceremonial hall which contains a 400m-square Hereke silk carpet. Here, Sultan Abdülhamit entertained Kaiser Wilhelm II in 1889 and 1898 and discussed matters of state. The **Yıldız Porcelain Factory** (Mon–Fri 9am–5pm; ₺20), downhill to the southeast of the Şale Pavilion, was established in 1890 to produce china for the palace and still churns out quantities of typically florid, nineteenth-century European-style pottery which is sold in the museum shop, should such wares appeal. There are a couple of decent cafés in the grounds, one housed in another of the palace's pavilions, the pretty **Malta Köşkü**. Also worth seeking out is the **Çadır Köşkü**, another charming pavilion downhill from the Malta Köşkü, beyond the small artificial lake.

Ortaköy

MAP P.114
Buses #22, #22/RE, #25/E from Kabataş, #40, #40/T, #42/T from Taksim.

Despite being dominated by the towering Bosphorus suspension bridge, built in 1973, and surrounded by urban sprawl, Ortaköy has not entirely lost its former fishing village charm. The waterfront area, the so-called boardwalk, is today all cool cafés frequented by well-heeled Istanbulites, who come to see and be seen – and perhaps browse the artsy-craftsy Sunday morning market. The waterfront mosque, the Büyük Mecidiye Camii, is a Baroque gem built in 1854, while in the streets behind are reminders of the village's cosmopolitan past, the (invariably locked) **Ezt Ahayim synagogue** and the attractive, nineteenth-century Greek Orthodox **church of Aya Fokas** (St Phocas), the door to the walled compound of which is occasionally open.

Baked potatoes in Ortaköy

Popular with hip, young clubbers by night and families by day (especially on Sundays), Ortaköy has a ready-made market for its latest culinary quirk – baked potatoes. Numerous stalls line the waterfront and side-streets selling red-hot varieties stuffed with virtually everything imaginable, from pungent Turkish cheeses and olives to spicy sausages and tuna.

Café

House Café

MAP P.114

Salhane Sok 1. Buses #25/E, #28, #40, #40/T, #42 ① 0212 227 2699, Ⓦ www. thehousecafe.com. Mon–Wed & Fri–Sun 8am–1am, Thurs 8.30am–1am.

A stylish, upmarket café whose concept has proven so popular there are now nine spread across the city. This has to be the best located, with views over the waterfront and Ortaköy's Baroque-style mosque, and it is housed in a lovingly converted turn-of-the-nineteenth-century building. Posh pastas, burgers and the like are the staple, Sunday brunch a metropolitan's favourite. Licensed.

Restaurants

Banyan

MAP P.114

Salhane Sok 3. Buses #25/E, #28, #40, #40/T, #42 ① 0212 259 9060, Ⓦ www. banyanrestaurant.com. Daily noon–2am.

Like its near neighbour and rival the *House Café*, this place

Banyan

concentrates on giving its loyal, largely youthful local clientele something a bit different, with Asian-fusion cuisine taking centre stage – from Indian to Vietnamese. It's not cheap (mains ₺32–95) but it's decent quality and the views of the Bosphorus Bridge and boardwalk are great. Licensed.

Hanedan

MAP P.114

Ciğdem Sok 27. Buses #25/E, #2,8 #40, #40/T, #42 ① 0212 260 4854, Ⓦ www. hanedanrestaurant.com. Daily 1am–midnight.

Established in 1983, this restaurant has a lively location next to Beşiktaş pier. The downstairs is given over to grilled meat dishes, the upstairs to seafood. There's a great selection of *meze* and a wide choice of fish, both farmed and wild caught. It's not as swish as some Bosphorus-front places and consequently better value, with fish sold by weight from ₺70 per kilo (enough for two). Licensed.

Tuğra

MAP P.114

Çırağan Palace Kempinski Hotel, Çırağan

Cad 32. Buses #25/E, #40, #40/T, #42
☎ 0212 236 7333, 🌐 www.kempinski.com.
Daily 7pm–midnight.

Appropriately expensive place located in this former palace, but worth it for the lovely Bosphorus views from the candle-lit terrace, attentive service and quality Ottoman-style dishes. Also in the *Çırağan Palace Kempinski* is the *Laledan* restaurant (same phone) noted for monumental breakfasts (300-plus items), Sunday brunches and seafood evening meals. Licensed.

Clubs & venues

IF Performance Hall

MAP P.114
Hasfirin Cad 26. ☎ 0546 566 9946, 🌐 www.ifperformance.com. Daily 9am–5am.

One of the best live music venues with architecture perfect for large concerts, being spacious and offering clear views of the stage from every point. The staff are very friendly, polite and caring. You can buy tickets either at the door or through 🌐 biletix.com, though make sure to check beforehand which of the two applies for a specific event. There are sometimes some sound issues in the smoking section.

Limoncello

MAP P.114
Süleyman Seba Cad 34. ☎ 0212 258 9822, 🌐 eksenistanbul.com. Tues–Sat 11pm–4am.

An urban, colourful and modern club with an intriguing, unique ambiance. The music tends to be half Turkish, half English-language. In the garden, the sound system is a little quiet. They have excellent cocktails with fresh fruit and some great desserts.

Sortie

MAP P.114
Muallım Nacı Cad 141/2. Buses #25/E, #28, #40, #40/T, #42 ☎ 0212 327 8585,

Tuğra

🌐 sortie.com.tr. Daily 6pm–4am. Admission Fri & Sat ₺90, weekdays free.

This sophisticated Bosphorus-front place plays a mix of house and pop, and though it has pretty steep admission fees at weekends you do get a drink on the house. As it's spread across 3500 square metres, there's plenty of room for Istanbul's fashionable elite to see and, more importantly, be seen. *Sortie* also attracts wealthy party animals from the Middle East and beyond. A series of nine themed restaurants – Mediterranean, sushi, South American, fish etc – are all part of the concept.

Supperclub

MAP P.114
Muallım Nacı Cad 65. Buses #25/E, #28, #40, #40/T, #42 ☎ 0212 261 1988, 🌐 supperclub-istanbul.business.site. Tues–Sun 11pm–5am. Admission Fri & Sat ₺60, weekdays free.

As one of two Turkish ventures by an Amsterdam-based group, this place might strike some as on the pretentious side. Expect to spend time lounging around on white sofas listening to local and international DJs mixing their stuff, and "spontaneous" performance art and video on occasion.

Asian Istanbul

Worth it for the bargain-priced ferry-ride from Europe to Asia alone, a few hours spent exploring conservative Üsküdar or bustling Kadıköy will enhance your Istanbul experience. The former of these suburbs, known to nineteenth-century visitors such as Florence Nightingale as Scutari, has several impressive Ottoman mosques within easy walking distance of the ferry terminal or Üsküdar Maramaray line metro stop as well as the Maiden's Tower, an offshore lighthouse that figured in Bond thriller *The World is Not Enough*. Kadıköy has transformed itself into a mini-Beyoğlu over the last few years and is great for shopping, eating and nightlife. It's also home to the pretty 1920s Süreyya Opera House and one of the city's best restaurants, *Çiya Sofrası*. Adjoining Kadıköy to the north is Haydarpaşa, with its imposing, early twentieth-century railway station, Florence Nightingale Museum and British Crimean War Cemetery.

Üsküdar and its Ottoman Mosques

MAP P.120, POCKET MAP N4
Regular ferries from Eminönü: Mon–Sat 6.30am–10pm; Sun 7.30am–10.30pm; last ferry back 10pm. ₺4 one-way. Marmaray line metro trains run under the Bosphorus from Sirkeci for ₺5.

Üsküdar ferry terminal is more or less opposite the **Mihrimah Camii**, built in 1547–1548. Like its namesake out by the city's land walls (see page 79), this fine mosque was designed for the favourite daughter of Süleyman the Magnificent, Mihrimah, by the skilled and prolific architect Sinan (see page 59). It was built on a raised terrace and is curious in design terms because, rather than using the conventional central dome flanked by two or four semi-domes, the Mihrimah Camii has three semi-domes. Around 500m to the southwest, on the far side of the Üsküdar stop of the trans-Bosphorus Marmaray metro line (see page 148), is

the very attractive **Şemsi Ahmet Paşa Camii**. Built in 1580, again a work of Sinan, it is set right on the water's edge. The tomb of the grand vizier for whom it was constructed, Şemsi Paşa, is located in the grounds. A little over half a kilometre inland, the **Yeni Valide Camii**, built at the behest of Ahmet III for his mother, was completed in 1710. Its most distinguished feature is the valide sultan's tomb, encased in an aviary-like mesh. Further inland is the **Atik Valide Külliyesi**, a mosque complex once again attributable to the ubiquitous Sinan, dating to 1583. Its courtyard is attractive and there's a small, traditional teahouse where you can sip sweet black tea with mosque-going regulars. Further east is the **Çinili Camii** and its associated hamam. Dating to 1640, the mosque is generally locked, but look helpless and the caretaker should appear to let you into the prayer hall. The historic **Çinili Hamamı** is just below

Getting around by ferry

Üsküdar's major sights are all within easy walking distance of the ferry terminal and Marmaray metro stop. Everything worth seeing or doing in Kadıköy lies just a short walk from the ferry terminal. But if you come for an evening meal or drink, double-check the times of the last ferry or metro back. Note that you can reach Kadıköy from Üsküdar by taking the Marmaray metro one stop to Ayrılık Çeşmesi then changing to the M4 metro for Kadıköy.

the mosque (Çavuşdere Cad 204 ☎ 0212 553 1593 men, 0216 334 9710 women, ⓦ www.cinilihamam. com; daily men 7am–10pm, women 8am–7.30pm; ₺30, extra ₺15 per scrub or massage). The building dates back to 1684, is clean without being antiseptic and the prices are a fraction of those in the old city's tourist-orientated bathhouses – but don't expect any English to be spoken. A taxi back to the waterfront is ₺8.

The Maiden's Tower (Kız Kulesi)

MAP P.120, POCKET MAP M4
Salacak. Museum Mon–Fri 9am–7pm, Sat & Sun 10am–7pm. ₺25.

A little over a kilometre south of the Üsküdar ferry terminal is a small pier where boats (Mon–Fri 9.15am–6.30pm; Sat & Sun 10am–6pm; ₺8 return) take visitors to the landmark tower. Also known as Leander's Tower, it was built in the fifth century BC to control ships using the Bosphorus. The Byzantines stretched a chain between it and another tower at the tip of the peninsula to block enemy ships and in the Ottoman era it became a lighthouse. There's a café and in the evenings a restaurant (7.30pm–1am) with a free private boat service (see ⓦ kizkulesi.com.tr.) to ferry diners to and fro. The views from the tower, up and down the Bosphorus and back across to the old city, are great.

Şemsi Ahmet Paşa Camii

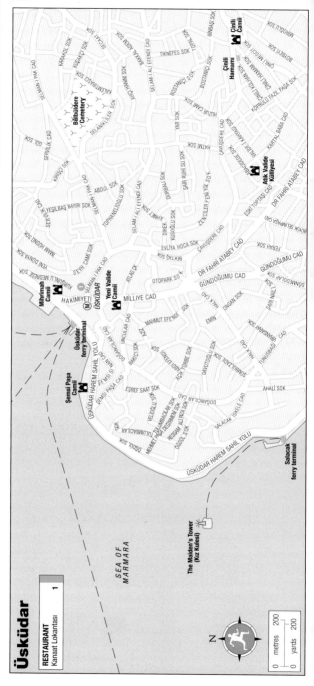

Üsküdar

RESTAURANT
Kanaat Lokantası   1

Kız Kulesi

Kadıköy

MAP P.122
Regular ferries from Eminönü Mon–Fri 7.35am–9.10pm, Sat & Sun 7.40am–9pm, last ferry back 8.30pm; from Karaköy 7am–11pm, last ferry back 8.30pm; both ₺4 one-way.

The heart of this lively suburb is south of the heaving waterfront, in the narrow grid of streets beyond Söğütlüçeşme Caddesi. Look out for older buildings among the more recent concrete ones, notably the cream curves of the Art Deco *Kurukhaveci Mehmet Efendi* coffee outlet. Pedestrianized **Güneşlibahçe Sokak** is well known for its quality delis and fruit, vegetable and fish stalls, and nearby a couple of churches, one Greek Orthodox, the other Armenian, attest to the area's cosmopolitan nineteenth-century past, when Istanbul's Christian minorities and foreigners lived here in numbers. Vaguely alternative clothing outlets mix with antique and bric-a-brac shops and there are some good restaurants, notably *Çiya Sofrası* (see page 124). Further inland is the beautiful **Süreyya Opera House** (Bahariye Cad 29 ℗ 0216 346 1531, ⓦ tinyurl.com/sureyya-operasi), a 1920s gem with a regular winter programme of opera, ballet and classical music. A little further east is the Rüştü Saraçoğlu stadium, home to Turkey's richest club, **Fenerbahçe**.

Toy Museum (Oyuncak Müzesi)

Dr Zeki Zeren Sok, Göztepe. Buses #GZ1, #GZ2, #10, #10/B from Kadıköy. ⓦ istanbuloyuncakmuzesi.com. Tues–Sun 9.30am–6pm. ₺15.

Appropriately housed in what was, until the 1950s, one of the city's best toyshops, this museum has a fine collection of toys drawn mainly from Western Europe and North America. Many exhibits are displayed in themed rooms, and there is everything here from teddy bears to Barbies, though best are the tin toys.

Kadıköy

CAFÉ	
Baylan	3
RESTAURANTS	
Çiya Sofrası	4
Fayton	1
Yanyalı	2

BARS	
Karga	3
Mila	1
Viktor Levi	2

SHOPS	
Brezilya	2
Sekerci Cafer Erol	1

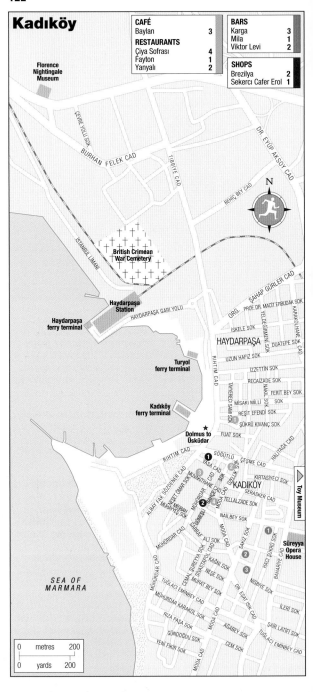

Florence Nightingale Museum

ÇEVRE YOLU SOK

BURHAN FELEK CAD

TIBBIYE CAD

DR. EYUP AKSOY CAD

BENIÇ BEY SOK

N

ISTANBUL LIMANI

British Crimean War Cemetery

ŞAHAP GÜRLER CAD

ORG. PROF. DR. MACIT ERBUDAK SOK

KARAKOLHANE CAD

Haydarpaşa Station

HAYDARPAŞA GARI YOLU

ISKELE SOK

YELDEĞIRMENI SOK

DUATEPE SOK

HAYDARPAŞA

Haydarpaşa ferry terminal

RIHTIM CAD

UZUN HAFIZ SOK

IZZETTIN SOK

RECAIZADE SOK

NAKIL SOK

FERIT BEY SOK

Turyol ferry terminal

TAYYERECI SAMI SOK

MISAKI MILLI SOK

REŞIT EFENDI SOK

ŞÜKRÜ KIVANÇ SOK

Kadıköy ferry terminal

FUAT SOK

HALITAĞA CAD

★ Dolmus to Üsküdar

SÖĞÜTLÜ

ÇEŞME CAD

RIHTIM CAD

YASA CAD

UZELLI SOK

KIRTASIYECI SOK

Toy Museum

ALBAY FAK. SÖZENER CAD

RESMET OMAR SOK

MUVAKITHANE CAD

MODA CAD

MÜHÜRDAR

ŞERBET ALI SOK

GÜNEŞLI SOK

MISBAH MUHAYYEŞ SOK

KADIKÖY

SERASKER CAD

TELLALZADE SOK

SIYASTPOL CAD

KAĞNI SOK

NAILBEY SOK

SAHIZ SOK

HACI ŞÜKRÜ SOK

BAHARIYE CAD

Süreyya Opera House

CEMAL SÜREYYA CAD

NEŞE SOK

MODA CAD

NISBIYE SOK

DR. ESAT ISIK CAD

İLERI SOK

SEA OF MARMARA

MÜHÜRDAR CAD

TUĞLACI EMINBEY CAD

MURAT BEY SOK

MÜHÜRDAR KARAKOL SOK

RIZA PAŞA SOK

GÜNDOĞDU SOK

YENI FIKIR SOK

MODA CAD

AĞABEY SOK

CEM SOK

ŞAIR LATIFEI SOK

TUĞLACI EMINBEY CAD

0	metres	200
0	yards	200

Haydarpaşa Station

MAP P.122

A handful of ferries from Karaköy call here – consult the timetables. ₺4 one-way.

Haydarpaşa station is well remembered by millions of Turks who arrived in the big city from villages and towns across Anatolia in the big waves of rural–urban migration between the 1950s and 1990s. German Gothic in style, it was built in 1908 as part of the ambitious Berlin-to-Baghdad railway, a gift from Kaiser Wilhelm II to Sultan Abdülhamit II, and is built on 1100 piles sunk into the Bosphorus. The station has been bypassed by the Marmaray metro project and its future is uncertain.

British Crimean War Cemetery

MAP P.122

TIBBİYE /Burhan Felek Cad, GATA yanı. Buses #12, #1/A from Kadıköy.

Attractively laid out beneath elegantly tapering cypress and spreading plane trees are the graves and tombs of some 6000 British soldiers who lost their lives in the Crimean War (1853–56). Most were victims of cholera which swept through the nearby military hospital in Scutari (today's Selimiye) barracks established by Florence Nightingale rather than battleground casualties. As well as victims of the Crimean War, there are over 700 civilians, and 450 Commonwealth soldiers from both world wars. The single most obvious monument is an obelisk decorated with four angels holding wreaths at each corner, erected at the behest of Queen Victoria in 1857. The cemetery, beautifully maintained by the Commonwealth War Graves Commission, is tricky to find on your own – it may be best to get a taxi in Kadıköy or Haydarpaşa. The entrance is by the *Acıl* (emergency) department of the GATA military hospital (*GATA Asker Hastanesi*).

Florence Nightingale Museum

MAP P.122

Kavak İskele Cad. Buses #12, #12/A from Kadıköy ⊕ 0216 553 1009, ⊕ 0216 310 7929 or ⊕ 0216 553 8000. Mon–Fri 9am–5pm. Free.

Housed in the monumental nineteenth-century Selimiye army barracks, strictly guarded by the Turkish military, this interesting museum can only be visited by applying at least 24 hours in advance – to be certain considerably more. Fax your passport details and expected date and time of arrival and hope for the best. The museum is actually on the site of the original hospital set up by Nightingale, in the northwest wing of the barracks, and contains two of the lamps she so famously used when doing her rounds. Although the cholera epidemic that swept through what was the world's first military hospital killed thousands (now buried in the British Crimean War Cemetery), it was here that Nightingale and her helpers established the precepts of modern nursing and eventually helped reduce the patient death rate from twenty to two percent.

Obelisk, British Crimean War Cemetery

Shops

Brezilya

MAP P.122
Guneşlibahçe Sok 21, Kadıköy. Daily 9am–9pm.

Much cheaper than the famed *Kurukhaveci Mehmet Efendi* coffee purveyors in Eminönü and Kadıköy, this place has been grinding coffee since 1920. It's also great for the healthy Turkish delicacy *pestil*, sheets of dried fruit molasses (usually apricot, grape, plum and mulberry) and other deli delights.

Şekerci Cafer Erol

MAP P.122
Yasa Cad 19, Kadıköy. ℹ 0216 337 1103, Ⓦ www.sekercicafererol.com. Daily 9am–midnight.

Even if you don't buy it's worth visiting this time-warp sweet shop for its wonderful window and counter displays, which accurately reflect the foundation date of this branch of the store in 1945 (though the family business has been going for over 200 years). Try the exquisitely attractive marzipan fruits, which in fact look far too precious to eat, or the more prosaic *alkide*, boiled sweets.

Şekerci Cafer Erol

Café

Baylan

MAP P.122
Muvakithane Cad 19, Kadıköy ℹ 0216 336 2881, Ⓦ baylangida.com. Daily 10am–10pm.

A relic of a bygone era but still going strong, this patisserie has a narrow, 1950s wood-and-chrome frontage and is famous for its eye-catching mini-macaroons, each a different pastel shade. There's respite from the hurly-burly outside in the vine-shaded garden. The perfect afternoon tea stop after a shopping expedition in Asia.

Restaurants

Çiya Sofrası

MAP P.122
Guneşlibahçe Sok 43, Kadıköy ℹ 0216 330 3190, Ⓦ www.ciya.com.tr. Daily 11am–10pm.

Offering one of the most varied menus in Istanbul this superb restaurant – actually three separate places either adjacent to or opposite each other on this pedestrianized street – Çiya has become a major incentive to visit the Asian side of the metropolis. Most popular at lunchtimes is the outlet on the

east side of the alley, where you choose from a tempting array of *meze*, salads and *sulu yemek* (stew-type dishes), and have your plate weighed to find out the damage – usually around ₺15–20. The two outlets on the other side of the street do superb kebabs. The dishes on offer are drawn from all over Turkey and adjacent Middle-Eastern countries. Unlicensed.

Fayton

MAP P.122
Tayyareci Sami Sok 2. ☎ 0216 346 0088. Daily 12am–1am.
This place used to be a blacksmith's shop and has been beautifully resorted and converted into a small, family-run restaurant. The cuisine is a mix of Greek and Turkish. A very pleasant, if a little intimate, place to have some homemade *meze* and a little raki. There's a mix of grilled dishes between ₺22 and 60 (the veal chop is the most expensive), you can try the fish soup for ₺20 and order some fresh fruit (₺5–10).

Kanaat Lokantası

MAP P.120, POCKET MAP O3
Selmanipak Cad 25, Üsküdar ☎ 0216 553 3791. Daily 7am–11pm.
Established back in 1931, this genteel *lokanta* makes a very worthwhile lunch-stop if you're exploring conservative Üsküdar's backstreets. There's a wide range of starters, both hot and cold, as well as a fantastic choice of mains (from ₺18) and desserts – many of them quite different to those found in the average Turkish restaurant – such as Circassian chicken in walnut sauce. Unlicensed.

Yanyalı

MAP P.122
Yağlıka İsmail Sok 1, Kadıköy ☎ 0216 336 3333. Daily 9am–10pm.
Similar to Üsküdar's *Kanaat* but even older, having been established by émigrés from Greece in 1919, it's not a place to come

for trendy, fusion cuisine – or even pizza or a burger. There are instead some twenty varieties of soup (₺8) on offer, a whole range of different stews including some oven-cooked in clay dishes, and a wide range of desserts including tahini-drenched candied pumpkin (*kabak tatlisi*). Unlicensed.

Bars

Karga

MAP P.122
Kadife Sok 16, Kadıköy ☎ 0216 449 1725. Daily 11am–2am.
Blurring the line between bar, alternative art gallery and café, this is where black-clad students and alternative-types come to drink beer, smoke (in the garden out back), chat and perhaps sample something from the bar-snack menu.

Mila

MAP P.122
Miralay Nazim Sok 6, Kadıköy ☎ 0216 405 2106, ⊛ mila-cafe-bar.business.site. Daily 10am–2am.
This is a charming, small, rustic wine bar hidden in one of Kadiköy's side streets. There's a very pleasant little backyard that you can enjoy your meal or wine in on a warm day. If there's a crowd, there may be a little wait for your food, but the friendliness of the staff will more than make up for it.

Viktor Levi

MAP P.122
Damacı Sok 4, Kadıköy ☎ 0216 449 9329. Daily 11am–2am.
Much more mainstream than *Karga*, *Viktor Levi* is housed in a substantial, late nineteenth-century house ranged around a pleasant garden. It's been making house wines since the 1920s and they are both reasonably priced and palatable enough. Extensive menu, too.

The Bosphorus and Princes' Islands

Few visitors to a city where the sea is so much a part of its being can resist the temptation of a boat trip up the Bosphorus. Over 31km long but a mere 700m wide at its narrowest point, the strait connects the Black and Marmara seas as well as separating Europe from Asia. Many of the impressive sights along the Bosphorus can be seen from the water; to explore them, the intrepid can take a bus from the city centre. The pretty Princes' Islands are just 35 minutes away by sea bus, a little longer by regular ferry. Here you can admire fin de siècle villas, ride in a horse-drawn carriage through pine-scented hills, hire a bike and, in summer, swim in the Sea of Marmara.

Bosphorus Cruises

The long, six-hour Bosphorus cruise run by Şehir Hatları (see page 147) is a highlight of any visit to Istanbul. Tickets (₺25 round trip) can be bought from the Boğaz Ferry Terminal just east of the Galata Bridge in Eminönü, with boats departing daily at

Bosphorus cruises, Rumeli Hisarı

10.35am year-round, 10.35am and 1.35pm May to September. An extra noon departure is usually added between June 9 and August 31. Drinks and snacks are available on board, as the only lengthy stop is a 2.5hr layover at peaceful Anadolu Kavağı village, on the strait's Asian side. En route, brief stops are made at Beşiktaş (Europe), Kanlıca (Asia), Sariyer and Rumeli Kavağı (both Europe). You can get off at any of these points (₺15 one-way tickets are available) but you'll have to take a bus back to the city centre. Travelling north, on the European shore you'll see Dolmabahçe Palace and Ortaköy before passing under the first Bosphorus Bridge, with **Beylerbeyi Palace** (see opposite) on the Asian shore virtually under the bridge. Back on the European side you'll pass **Arnavutköy** and **Bebek**, once sleepy fishing villages turned prosperous suburbs. Before the second bridge rises, you'll see the landmark **Rumeli Hisarı** fortress (see page 128) and on the Asian side a good example of a *yalı* (Ottoman-era waterfront

Borusan Contemporary

mansion), the **Köprülü
Amcazade Hüesyin Paşa Yalı**.
Beyond the second bridge is the
Sakıp Sabancı Museum (see
page 128). Try the sugared
yoghurt brought on by vendors at
Kanlıca, then on the European
side look out for **Sait Halim Paşa
Yalı** at Yeniköy, an Art Nouveau
delight. Sariyer is home to the
Sadberk Hanım Museum (see
page 129). The strait becomes
less built up as you approach the
layover point at **Anadolu Kavağı**,
where most visitors are content
to stretch their legs and enjoy a
cheap fish meal in green, quiet
surroundings, though there's a
Byzantine fortress to clamber up
to for the energetic.

Other cruises include Şehir
Hatları's short tour from Eminönü
to Ortaköy departing daily at
2.30pm (t12 round trip) and
private operator Turyol has 1.5hr-
long tours up to the second, Fatih
Mehmet Sultan, bridge at least
hourly between 10am and 9pm,
more frequently summer weekends
(t12 round trip). Alternatively from
mid-June to the end of September
only there's a Şehir Hatları

Saturday-night cruise (Mehtaplı)
departing Eminönü at 6.35pm (t20
round trip), which goes as far as
Anadolu Kavağı.

Beylerbeyi Palace

MAP P.128
Abdullah Ağa Cad 12. Buses #15, #15/B
from Üsküdar ☎ 0216 321 9320. Tues–Sun
9am–5pm. t40.

An even grander take on the grand
yalıs (waterfront mansions) lining
the Bosphorus, this nineteenth-
century marble pile was the
summer residence and guesthouse
of late Ottoman sultans. Entrance
is expensive, but if European-
style palace architecture is your
thing it may appeal – and it has
attractive gardens.

Borusan Contemporary

MAP P.128
Perili Köşk, 5 Hisar Cad. Buses #40, and
#40/T from Taksim, #22, #22/RE and
#25/E from Kabataş. ☎ 0212 3935 200,
Ⓦ borusancontemporary.com. Sat & Sun
10am–9pm. t10.

This unique contemporary
arts centre operates as the
headquarters of Borusan
Holdings during the week, but

is open on Saturday and Sunday for art lovers, with all kinds of installations, sculptures and photographs. The building itself, in the shadow of the second Bosphorus Bridge, is a striking ten-storey brick-built mansion begun in 1910, which soon became known as the Perili Köşk ("Haunted Mansion").

Rumeli Hisarı

MAP P.128

Yahya Kemal Cad 42. Buses #22, #25/E, #40, #40/T ☎ 0212 263 5305. Mon & Tues, Thurs–Sun 9.30am–5pm. ₺10.

Superb fortification of six towers joined by curtain walling just before the second suspension bridge (Fatih Sultan Mehmet), Rumeli Hisarı was built in 1452 as part of Sultan Mehmet's plans to capture Constantinople. Working in tandem with the **Anadolu Hisarı** fort, still visible across the strait in Asia, it effectively blocked the Bosphorus to enemy ships and cut off aid to the beleaguered Byzantines.

Sakıp Sabancı Museum

MAP P.128

Sakıp Sabancı Cad. Buses #22, #25/E, #40, #40/T ☎ 0212 277 2200, ⓦ sakipsabancimuzesi.org. Tues & Thurs–Sun 10am–6pm, Weds 10am–8pm. ₺30.

Housed in a beautifully restored 1920s waterfront villa, this superb museum-cum-gallery hosts major exhibitions, which in the past have included the likes of Dalí and Picasso. In addition there's a good permanent collection of Ottoman-era calligraphy and works by nineteenth- and twentieth-century Turkish artists. Just up the waterfront is **Emirgan Parkı** (daily 8am–5pm), the city's most attractive park, with some lovely turn-of-the-century pavilions and fine stands of tulips in April.

THE BOSPHORUS AND PRINCES' ISLANDS

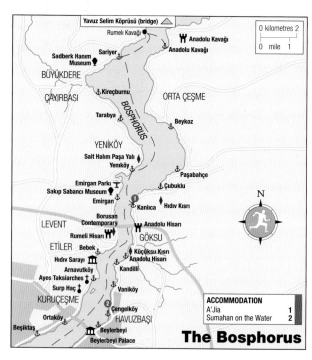

ACCOMMODATION
A'Jia — 1
Sumahan on the Water — 2

The Bosphorus

Sakıp Sabancı Museum

Sadberk Hanım Museum

MAP P.128

Büyükdere Cad 27–29. Buses #25/E, #40, #40/T ☎ 0212 242 3813, ⊕ www. sadberkhanimmuzesi.org.tr. Daily except Wed 10am–5pm. ₺10.

This pair of turn-of-the-nineteenth-century waterfront houses have been lovingly converted into a satisfying museum. The house on the right as you enter is given over to mainly Ottoman-period artefacts, including some fine ceramics, as well as rooms mocked-up as they would have been in the nineteenth century. The house on the left is home to a private collection of small but top-quality artefacts collected from Anatolia, from Urartian bronze work to Attic red-figure vases and Hellenistic gold jewellery to Roman figurines.

Kınalıada

MAP P.130

Ferries and sea buses dock at the island's sole settlement on the east coast, where there are plenty of cafés and restaurants. There's little to see on this rather barren outcrop, bar the church of **Surp Krikor Lusavoriç**, up the hill behind the waterfront. Built in 1857, it is notable for its windows, painted nostalgically with famous churches from the Armenians' homeland in what is now Eastern Turkey. The Istanbul Armenians, who make up most of the island's (mainly summer-only) community, keep this symbol of their faith in immaculate condition. The island takes its Turkish name Kınalıada or "Henna Island" from its red cliffs. You can bike around the island too.

Burgazada

MAP P.130

Again essentially a single settlement clustering around the ferry terminal, Burgazada is green and partially forested. The little town is dotted with some nice wooden villas, mostly shrouded by oleander, fig and palm trees, and is home to the large, nineteenth-century Greek Orthodox **Church of St John the Baptist**. Also in the backstreets you'll find the **Sait Faik Museum** on Burgaz Çayırı Sok 15 (☎ 0216 381 2060; Wed–Sat 10.30am–5pm; free). The house of Sait Faik, a bohemian whose short stories chronicled the harsh lives of the poor, has been well preserved. If you're feeling energetic, hire a bike and explore – one worthwhile stop is **Kalpazankaya**, where you can swim and eat in a decent restaurant of the same name. Alternatively, ride here in a horse-drawn carriage (phaeton; *fayton* in Turkish) as part of an island tour (from ₺45). There's decent accommodation at *Mehtap 45* (see page 140).

Heybeliada

MAP P.130

Larger and more popular as a day or weekend outing than either Kınalıada or Burgazada, this attractive island gets its name Heybeliada or "**Island of the Saddlebag**", from the twin hills that dominate it. The small settlement where the ferry docks, on the east coast, has numerous pretty fin de siècle villas, including one where the family of novelist Orhan Pamuk (see page 100) summered. Again, there are plenty of places to eat and drink in town and a limited choice of places to stay (see page 140). In town

is an imposing **Naval School** (Deniz Harp Okulu) and the Greek Orthodox **Church of Aya Nikola**, curiously adorned with a clock tower. Like all the islands, it's traffic-free so the best way to get around is by phaeton (tours start from Ayyıldız Caddesi behind the waterfront), though a bicycle hired from one of several outlets near the jetty works out much cheaper and gives much more flexibility. Best of the three beach clubs is **Değirmen Burnu Plajı** (9am–dusk; ₺15 weekdays, ₺20 Sat & Sun) on the northwest coast, a shingle strip at the foot of cliffs in a pine forest.

Büyükada

MAP P.130

This is by far the most visited of the Princes' Islands. The visitors milling around the ferry terminal of the main settlement can be off-putting, but hire a bike or walk and you're soon away from

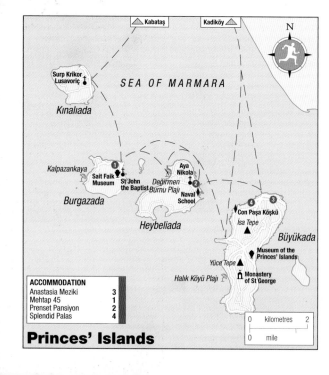

Princes' Islands

Getting to the Princes' Islands

In Byzantine times home to monasteries and banished royalty, and at the turn of the nineteenth century to the city's wealthy Christian minorities, the islands today (Adalar in Turkish) are a popular escape. The jump-off point is Eminönü quay, from where **Şehir Hatları** ferries run nine times a day to the four main islands for ₺5.5 one way, ₺4.4 with İstanbulkart (see page 145). The ferries from Eminönü stop at Kadıköy on the Asian shore before continuing to the islands. Several companies operate smaller boats for a slightly higher price. All of these boats take around an hour and a half to reach Büyükada, the biggest island, and fifty minutes to the smallest and nearest, Kınalıada. Turyol boats run from Karaköy, Denturavrasya from Beşiktaş. The fast IDO sea buses that used to run from Kabataş to the islands no longer run owing to the redevelopment of the Kabataş dock. It was rumoured that the project had been abandoned, however, the Istanbul Metropolitan Municipality denied this and stated that the project will be completed eventually.

the crowds. The most sumptuous of the islands' wooden mansions, once owned by wealthy Jewish and Greek families, are on Büyükada, many on the shore west of the Art Nouveau **Splendid Palas** hotel (see page 140). One roofless and abandoned house below the splendid wooden mansion **Con Paşa Köşkü**, on Çankaya Caddesi, was home to **Trotsky**, who started the *History of the Russian Revolution* while exiled here between 1929 and 1933. Again, you can explore by phaeton or bicycle (try Trek on Nisan Cad 23, behind the clock tower), with a round island trip taking about an hour and a half. There's plenty to see, not least the **Monastery of St George** (usually open; free) on **Yüce Tepe**, a prominent pine-covered hill. It's about a fifteen-minute walk to the summit and bikes are not allowed. On the east of the island the **Museum of the Princes' Islands** (March–Nov Tues–Sun 9am–6pm; Dec–Feb 10am–5pm; ₺5) has an exhibition about the island's writers and poets and nearby is the charming boutique *Ayanikola Butik* hotel. There are several places to swim; by far the most peaceful

is the **Halik Köyü Plajı** (8am–dusk; ₺15), reached by steep steps from the road running around the island some 3km south of the town. Many views from the islands inevitably at least partially include the urban sprawl of the metropolis, but here you have lovely views across the Sea of Marmara to its distant, wooded south shore.

Phaeton

ACCOMMODATION

Kybele Hotel

Accommodation

Accommodation is rarely in short supply, especially following the downturn in tourism owing to security concerns (see page 137). Most visitors choose to stay around Sultanahmet, the heart of the old city, where there is a high concentration of hotels, pensions and hostels, as well as major sights. Inevitably given the demand, many establishments have opened on the fringes of Sultanahmet – in Sirkeci and towards the Grand Bazaar. Ever more visitors, particularly those for whom nightlife and contemporary arts and culture are as important as historical sights, are basing themselves across the Golden Horn in trendy Galata and Beyoğlu. If you're looking for exclusivity, a pricey Bosphorus-front hotel may well appeal, while those looking to spend a night on an island retreat may be tempted by the Princes' Islands.

Sultanahmet

AGORA GUEST HOUSE & HOSTEL MAP P.26, POCKET MAP H12. Amiral Tafdil Sok 6 ⊕ 1 Sultanahmet ☎ 0212 458 5547, Ⓦ agoraguesthouse.com. A hip and successful cross between a guesthouse and hostel in a quiet street off busy Akbıyık Caddesi, one of its best points is the stylish communal lounge fronted by a terrace. There are ten en-suite double rooms and dorms ranging from four- to ten-beds – including one female-only. The one downside is the small number of shared bathrooms. **Dorms from €16, doubles €80**

ALP MAP P.26, POCKET MAP J12. Akbıyık Cad, Adliye Sok 4 ⊕ 1 Sultanahmet ☎ 0212 517 7067, Ⓦ alpguesthouse. com. Period-style hotel down a quiet alley off bustling, tourist-central Akbıyık Caddesi. The rooms are on the small side but tastefully done-out with wood floors, rugs, pale walls with dark-wood trim – and some have four-poster beds. The partly enclosed roof terrace has good views of the entrance to the Bosphorus, as do a few of the rooms. **€55**

CHEERS MAP P.26, POCKET MAP H10. Zeynepsultan Camii Sok 21 ⊕ 1 Sultanahmet ☎ 0212 526 0200, Ⓦ cheershostel.com. More subtle than its Sultanahmet rivals, this hostel is nicely located on a quiet side street in a characterful early twentieth-century house. It has a range of well-kitted-out rooms, from doubles to four- and ten-bed dorms. One major plus is the upstairs bar, with a terrace affording a picture-postcard view of the Haghia Sophia. Friendly and well managed, too. **Dorms from €18, doubles €49**

CHEERS LIGHTHOUSE MAP P.26, POCKET MAP G9. Çayıroğlu Sok 18 ⊕ 1 Sultanahmet ☎ 0212 458 2324, Ⓦ cheershostel.com. Part of a new wave of hostel accommodation in the city, it provides hotel-like facilities without losing the communal hostel feel. The five rooms here range from a six-bed dorm to a luxury penthouse, with some facing a quiet street, others the sea, a stone's throw away across the defunct suburban railway line. There's free wi-fi and coffee and an excellent in-house restaurant. **Dorms from €12, penthouse suite €120**

DENİZ HOUSES MAP P.26, POCKET MAP G9. Çayıroğlu Sok 14 ⊕ 1 Sultanahmet ☎ 0212 518 9595, Ⓦ denizhouses.com. Two adjoining period buildings, down a quiet alley below the major concentration of hotels on and around Akbıyık Caddesi, make up this well-run establishment. Rooms in A block are small but homely, with stripped wood floors and Turkish rugs. Front rooms have sea views but get some noise from the suburban railway below. B Block rooms are larger and quieter but there are no sea views – go up to the pleasant roof terrace for these. €50

EMPRESS ZOE MAP P.26, POCKET MAP J12. Akbıyık Cad, Adliye Sok 10 ⓣ 1 Sultanahmet ⓣ 0212 518 2504, ⓦ emzoe. com. You can't get much more historic than a hotel built over the remains of an Ottoman bathhouse, which itself stands on the basement wall of a Byzantine palace. The American owners have stamped their distinctive mark on this treasure of a boutique hotel which, despite the rather small rooms and tricky layout, makes for a wonderfully atmospheric stay in the heart of the old city. €110

FOUR SEASONS SULTANAHMET MAP P.26, POCKET MAP H12. Tevfikhane Sok 1 ⓣ 1 Sultanahmet ⓣ 0212 638 8200, ⓦ fourseasons.com For anyone with a desire to spend a night in a former prison (*not* the one Billy Hayes was incarcerated in *Midnight Express*), this luxury hotel may fit in the bill. The rooms are palatial, with all the mod-cons you'd expect. The Neoclassical architecture is splendid, the situation excellent – it backs, controversially, onto Byzantine substructures being turned into an "archeology park" – and you don't have to slop out. €344

HANEDAN MAP P.26, POCKET MAP J12. Akbıyık Cad, Adliye Sok 3 ⓣ 1 Sultanahmet ⓣ 0212 516 4869, ⓦ hanedanhotel.com. This is one of the best affordable hotels in Cankurtaran, run by a knowledgeable partnership of four friends. The standard rooms have king-sized beds sitting on dark wooden boards, pastel-coloured walls and dark wood furniture. The triple and family rooms have four-poster beds and there are good views from the roof terrace. €37

İBRAHİM PAŞA MAP P.26, POCKET MAP G12. Terzihane Sok 5 ⓣ 1 Sultanahmet ⓣ 0212 518 0395, ⓦ ibrahimpasha.com. Superb blend of old and new in this lovingly converted pair of nineteenth-century townhouses, quietly located just off the Hippodrome. Bare boards, tasteful rugs and a successful blend of antique furniture and contemporary fittings are the basics of the mix of standard and deluxe rooms. Fabulous roof terrace with sweeping sea and old city views, a charming lounge with open fire downstairs and friendly, professional staff. €145

KYBELE MAP P.26, POCKET MAP G11. Yerebatan Cad 35 ⓣ 1 Sultanahmet ⓣ 0212 511 7766, ⓦ kybelehotel.com. One of the old city's first boutique hotels run by three outgoing brothers, the *Kybele* has been fashioned from a distinctive

Getting a room

All prices are for the cheapest double room in high season, which for most establishments is mid-March to mid-November and Christmas/New Year – though many places have reductions in July and August. Low-season rates are usually fifteen to twenty percent less. Don't be afraid to ask for a reduction – bargaining is part of the culture – and some smaller places will offer a discount (between five and ten percent) for payment in cash.

Breakfast is included in all places listed except apartments; the vast majority have air conditioning to cope with the city's sultry summers, and double glazing and central heating for the sometimes cold, damp winters. Free wi-fi is also a given in all but the more expensive chain hotels. Istanbul is an international city, and the vast majority of hotels quote their prices in euros to reflect their clientele.

rendered-brick terraced house. Forget it if minimalism is your thing because this place is crammed with vintage artefacts and has over 4000 antique/period-style light fittings. The sixteen rooms have brass beds and stripped wood floors, while out back is a quiet garden and reading area. **€80**

NOMADE MAP P.26, POCKET MAP G11. Ticarethane Sok 15 ⓣ 1 Sultanahmet ⓣ 0212 569 2727, ⓦ hotelnomade. tr. One of the old city's few designer boutique hotels, the *Nomade* is run by twin sisters who have given their prodigy a distinctive stamp – white floors, striking colour schemes, blonde wood contemporary furniture mixed with ethnic artefacts. Great roof-terrace bar, too, with superb views of the Haghia Sophia. **€75**

OTTOMAN HOTEL IMPERIAL MAP P.26, POCKET MAP H11. Caferiye Sok 6/1 ⓣ 1 Sultanahmet ⓣ 0212 513 6151, ⓦ ottomanhotelimperial.com. A well-run period-style hotel right in the heart of Sultanahmet, offering a wide range of plush rooms conservatively kitted-out with dark wood furniture and shiny bedspreads. The views from the premium rooms especially are stunning, with the magnificent Haghia Sophia dominating the scene. Attached is the *Matbah* restaurant (see page 40), well known for its Ottoman cuisine. **€231**

PENINSULA MAP P.26, POCKET MAP J12. Adliye Sok 6 ⓣ 1 Sultanahmet ⓣ 0212 4586850, ⓦ hotelpeninsula.com. A small double here is less than one in many of the city's hostels, so it's a good budget option. Newly built in traditional style, it sticks largely to the convention hereabouts of bare floor (laminate in this case), pastel walls and vaguely Ottoman-period decor. Tidy bathrooms and a range of rooms from small singles to a two-room family suite. **€35**

SİDE HOTEL & PENSION MAP P.26, POCKET MAP H12. Utangaç Sok 20 ⓣ 1 Sultanahmet ⓣ 0212 517 2282, ⓦ sidehotel.com. A hybrid pension-cum-hotel, this place has been getting good reviews since 1989 – due in no small part to the very friendly trio of brothers who run it. Rooms in the hotel section are en suite and have air conditioning, those on the

pension side rely on fans for cooling. The six rooms on the upper floor have (spotless) shared bathrooms. The pension rooms are better value than the hotel. **Pension €40, hotel €60**

SULTAN HOSTEL MAP P.26, POCKET MAP H12. Akbıyık Cad 21 ⓣ 1 Sultanahmet ⓣ 0212 516 9260, ⓦ sultanhostel.com. The city's biggest hostel and main rival to the equally mammoth *Orient* virtually next door, it offers a wide range of rooms, from doubles to a 26-bed dorm. It's got a good reputation for cleanliness and the friendliness of its staff. Dorm rooms are good value but you can find doubles in pensions nearby for the same, or even less, money. **Dorms €19, doubles €33**

TURKOMAN MAP P.26, POCKET MAP G12. Asmalı Çeşme Sok 2 ⓣ 1 Sultanahmet ⓣ 0212 516 2956, ⓦ turkomanhotel.com. Right opposite the Egyptian Obelisk on the Hippodrome, this long-established boutique hotel, housed in a tall, narrow nineteenth-century building, has bags of character. All the rooms have brass beds, stripped boards and high ceilings, and there's a pleasant roof terrace for breakfast, with views across to the Blue Mosque. **€75**

UYAN MAP P.26, POCKET MAP H12. Utangaç Sok 2 ⓣ 1 Sultanahmet ⓣ 0212 518 9255, ⓦ uyanhotel.com. This is one of the more stylish mid-range options in the heart of Sultanahmet, and the rooms in this converted 1920s corner-plot residence are bright, light and clean (bar ground-floor rooms) with white walls, light wood floors and crisp, white bed linen. There are good views of the Haghia Sophia from the roof terrace, while suite-room 405 is named the "Blue Mosque Room" for obvious reasons. **€81**

WHITE HOUSE MAP P.26, POCKET MAP G11. Çatalçeşme Sok 21 ⓣ 1 Sultanahmet ⓣ 0212 526 0019, ⓦ istanbulwhitehouse. com. On the north side of the main tramline, this beautifully appointed hotel won't suit those looking for a genuine period or boutique hotel – but it's hard to beat for reliable comfort. Rooms are faux-Ottoman, all patterned wallpapers, cream, gilt, ornate furniture and bold bedspreads. Breakfasts

Rates slashed

Following a series of terrorist attacks in 2016 and early 2017 (see page 151), the number of tourists visiting the city dropped considerably. The previously buoyant tourism industry had led to artificially high rates, and faced with stiff competition for the reduced numbers of guests, many hotels were forced to slash their prices by as much as half. Some also went out of business. When things return to normal in this vibrant city, it's likely that prices will rise to their previous levels quickly – the prices quoted here may be on the low side.

are excellent and views from the roof terrace are expansive. **€159**

Topkapı Palace to the Golden Horn

NEORION MAP P.44, POCKET MAP G6. Orhaniye Cad 14 🚋 1 Sultanahmet ☎ 0212 527 9090, Ⓦ neorionhotel.com. There's nothing particularly flash about this 53-room establishment, but its staff go to considerable lengths to keep their guests happy. There is a roof terrace where you can enjoy a free drink each night while you gaze across the Bosphorus, as well as a free basement pool, Jacuzzi, sauna and Turkish bath. Rooms are kept pristine, and have subtle Ottoman-style decor as well as LCD TVs. **€139.**

SİRKECİ MANSION MAP P.44, POCKET MAP H6. Taya Hatun Cad 5 🚋 1 Gülhane ☎ 0212 528 4344, Ⓦ sirkecimansion. com. Tucked away down a side street off the main tramline and overlooking the walls of Gülhane Park, this popular hotel is impeccably run. The rooms are comfortable without being overly ornate, there's a fitness centre in the basement and nice touches like free afternoon tea and cake for guests. The roof terrace commands grand vistas over the park and Topkapı Palace beyond. **€131**

Grand Bazaar and around

NILES MAP P.60, POCKET MAP E8. Dibekli Camii Sok 13 🚋 1 Beyazıt ☎ 0212 517 3239, Ⓦ hotelniles.com. Good-value hotel on a steep street running down to the sea from the tramline and just a few

minutes' walk from the Grand Bazaar. This area is more workaday than Sultanahmet, a real bonus if you want to be a little away from your fellow visitors. The standard rooms are smallish, but there's a green and pleasant patio garden plus a roof terrace with sea views. **€75**

PRESIDENT (BEST WESTERN) MAP P.60, POCKET MAP E8. Tiyatro Cad 25 🚋 1 Beyazıt ☎ 0212 516 6980, Ⓦ thepresidenthotel.com. Better-than-average large, chain hotel just minutes from the Grand Bazaar and handy for the Beyazıt tram. There's a range of different rooms, from standard doubles and twins to suites, and the decor is restrained. Those with Sea of Marmara views carry a premium. The circular, year-round rooftop pool is a plus for some, as is the gym. **€91**

The Northwest quarter

KARİYE MAP P.74, POCKET MAP A2. Kariye Camii Sok 6 🚍 1 Ulubatlı ☎ 0212 534 8414. This fine period hotel is out of the way and a visit to Sultanahmet requires a metro and a tram ride, but it is in a fascinating area – right next to the land walls and the superb Kariye Museum (see page 72). As it's one of the first Istanbul mansion houses that were converted into hotels, it's showing a few signs of wear and tear but is extremely good value – plus it's got one of the city's best restaurants, *Asitane* (see page 83), attached. **€70**

TROYA HOTEL BALAT MAP P.74, POCKET MAP C3. Abdülezelpaşa Cad 97 ☎ 0212 531 4858, Ⓦ troyahotelbalat.com. The narrow, steep and twisting streets of nineteenth-century houses in up-and-coming Fener and adjoining Balat, and the Golden Horn waterfront views, make this hotel a great place to stay off the beaten track. The place oozes nineteenth-century Greek style, with original period murals in most rooms, solid wooden doors, stripped wood floors and vintage furniture. Hearty buffet breakfast too. The only drawback is traffic noise from the road running alongside the Golden Horn. **€60**

Galata

10 KARAKÖY MAP P.86, POCKET MAP B15. Kemeraltı Cad 10 ⊙ 0212 703 3333, Ⓦ morganshotelgroup.com/originals. This fine late nineteenth-century Neoclassical building has been given a superb makeover by renowned architect Sinan Kafadar. There's a tempting mix of standard, luxury and roof suite rooms, as well as a very sophisticated terrace bar and a slow-food-orientated dining room downstairs. Doubles from **€139**

ANEMON GALATA MAP P.86, POCKET MAP A15. Büyükhendek Cad 11 Ⓜ 2 Şişhane or Tünel İstiklal ⊙ 0212 293 2343, Ⓦ anemonhotels.com. With an excellent location on the square at the foot of the landmark Galata Tower, this place is in the heart of the district's bohemian action. The hotel itself is part of a chain, however, with mock Art Nouveau/Victoriana-style decor and maximum comfort – including tubs in the bathrooms. **€100**

SUB KARAKÖY MAP P.86, POCKET MAP C14. Necatibey Cad 9 ⊙ 0212 243 0005, Ⓦ subkarakoy.com. A very apt hotel for hip Karaköy, this stylish place with a trendy crow motif has a select number of individually designed and furnished rooms, each with a modern bathroom with rain shower and high-quality toiletries. It also has a great terrace bar with an excellent range of local wines available, as well as a wholesome whole-food breakfast which is dished-up downstairs. **€240**

VAULT KARAKÖY MAP P.86, POCKET MAP A15. Bankalar Cad 5, Karaköy Ⓜ 1 Karaköy or Tünel Karaköy ⊙ 0212 244 6434, Ⓦ thehousehotel.com. Occupying an imposing former bank building dating

back to 1863, this hotel has been converted into a hotel by one of Istanbul's leading architects, Sinan Kafadar. Original features abound, including subtly patterned granite floors, high ceilings and the vaults themselves. South-facing rooms have great views over the Golden Horn, and rooms have mod-cons like big-screen LCD TVs. Part of the well-regarded House brand. **€147**

WORLD HOUSE HOSTEL MAP P.86, POCKET MAP B14. Galipdede Cad 85 Ⓜ 1 Şişhane or Tünel İstiklal ⊙ 0212 293 5520, Ⓦ worldhouseistanbul.com. For a rock-bottom stay this side of the Golden Horn, this hostel is very hard to beat. The rooms are kept spotless but are a little spartan, and its excellent location on happening Galipdede Caddesi is only tempered slightly by the loud call to prayer from the next-door mosque each morning. **Dorms €14, doubles €58**

Beyoğlu

BÜYÜK LONDRA MAP P.96, POCKET MAP B12. Meşrutiyet Cad 117 Ⓜ 2 Şişhane or Tünel İstiklal ⊙ 0212 249 1025, Ⓦ londrahotel.net. The lowest priced rooms in this once extremely grand **fin de siècle** hotel are as cheap as you'll find in any part of the city you'd want to stay in, and despite the tiny bathrooms and slightly worn decor, they're more than adequate. The real pull here, though, is the location, time-warp bar (see page 108), roof bar and general untouched, period ambience. There's a decent breakfast, too. **€50**

DEVMAN MAP P.96, POCKET MAP B13. Asmalımescit Sok 52 Ⓜ 2 Şişhane or Tünel İstiklal ⊙ 0212 245 6212, Ⓦ devmanhotel. com. Among a slew of cheapish options on bustling Asmalimescit Sokak, a narrow alley lined with *meyhanes* and bars, this is a great option if you're looking for basic, no-frills but clean accommodation, right in the thick of the nightlife and shopping. Can be noisy, especially on weekend nights. **€40**

MARMARA PERA MAP P.96, POCKET MAP A13. Meşrutiyet Cad 21 Ⓜ 2 Şişhane or Tünel İstiklal ⊙ 0212 251 4646, Ⓦ themarmarahotels.com. A twelve-storey high-rise towering over neighbouring nineteenth-century apartment blocks and hotels, this smart establishment has stylishly modern rooms and a rooftop pool and bar with sensational views, as well as the popular *Mikla* restaurant (see page 107). **€199**

PERA PALACE MAP P.96, POCKET MAP A13. Meşrutiyet Cad 52 Ⓜ 2 Şişhane or Tünel İstiklal ☏ 0212 377 4000, Ⓦ perapalace.com. This historic hotel (see page 98) trades on its respectable reputation, so you can expect to pay a hefty premium to stay in its refurbished rooms. That said, some of them were occupied in grander times past by the likes of Agatha Christie and Ernest Hemingway. **€162**

RICHMOND HOTEL MAP P.96, POCKET MAP B13. İstiklal Cad 227 Ⓜ 2 Şişhane or Tünel İstiklal ☏ 0212 252 5460, Ⓦ richmondhotels.com.tr. Not the most stylish hotel in Beyoğlu, this is nonetheless a reliable mid-range option, with standard rooms conservatively done out in neutrals. It is well located right on İstiklal Caddesi, some upper rear rooms have great Bosphorus views (at a premium) and there's the cool *Leb-i-Derya* bar-restaurant (see page 109). **€116**

TOM TOM SUITES MAP P.96, POCKET MAP B13.Boğazkesen Cad, Tomtom Kaptan Sok 18 Ⓜ 2 Şişhane or Tünel İstiklal ☏ 0212 292 4949, Ⓦ tomtomsuites. com. Located opposite the beautiful nineteenth-century Italian Consulate, this similarly dated property offers a superbly presented series of suites, all subtle whites and soft browns. It's hard to know what the Franciscan nuns who once called this place home would have made of the underfloor heated bathrooms and Jacuzzis. **€131**

TRİADA RESIDENCE MAP P.96, POCKET MAP D11. İstiklal Cad, Meşelik Sok 4 Ⓜ 2 Taksim ☏ 0212 251 0101. Pretty boutique hotel converted from a grand period dwelling on a narrow alley off İstiklal Caddesi, overlooking the Aya Triada church (see page 100). The large (40 square metre) rooms are very stylish and all have an American-style kitchen with a coffee-making machine and fridge – and there's also a wonderful roof terrace. **€90**

VILLA ZURICH MAP P.96, POCKET MAP D13. Akarsu Yokuşu Cad 36, Ⓜ 2 Taksim ☏ 0212 293 0604, Ⓦ hotelvillazurich.com. This is a well-established, traditional hotel located in the backstreets of now trendy Cihangir, with large, well-equipped double rooms. There's a smart rooftop terrace where you can eat a substantial breakfast while admiring the views across the Bosphorus. **€57**

Beşiktaş and Ortaköy

ÇIRAĞAN PALACE KEMPİNSKİ MAP P.114. Çırağan Cad 32. Buses #25/E, #28, #40, #40/T, #42/T ☏ 0212 326 4646, Ⓦ kempinski.com. As opulent as you'd imagine from a hotel fashioned from a Bosphorus-front, European-style Ottoman palace (see page 113). There's a huge outdoor pool, several restaurants and the inevitable designer boutiques. Every room has a balcony and the decor is a safe blend of the traditional and contemporary. **€368**

FOUR SEASONS BOSPHORUS MAP P.114. Çırağan Cad 28. Buses #25/E, #28, #40, #40/T, #42/T ☏ 0212 381 4000, Ⓦ fourseasons.com. Like rival the *Çırağan Palace Kempinski*, this upmarket chain hotel is set in a former palace on the Bosphorus and offers similar levels of comfort and luxury. The rooms and suites are very elegant and most have fabulous Bosphorus views – and there's a great pool and Turkish bath. **€468**

LES OTTOMANS MAP P.114. Muallim Naci Cad 68. Buses #25/E, #28, #40, #40/T, #42/T ☏ 0212 359 1500, Ⓦ lesottomans. com. This is a beautiful hotel that was once a grand *yalı* (waterfront mansion), but prices here make the *Four Seasons* and *Kempinski* look like budget options. This is the last word in exclusive luxury on the Bosphorus, so you probably wouldn't want to arrive here by one of the public buses listed above. **€720**

W HOTEL MAP P.114. Süleyman Seba Cad 22. Buses #25/E, #28, #40, #40/T, #42/T ☏ 0212 381 2121, Ⓦ whotels. com/istanbul. Upmarket, self-consciously hip chain hotel, the *W* in Beşiktaş is appropriately set in the posh Akaretler shopping centre – no mere mall, but a series of period townhouses converted into boutiques and the like. Aimed largely at prosperous men up for some sophisticated clubbing and shopping. **€149**

Bosphorus and Princes' Islands

A'JİA MAP P.128. Çubuklu Cad 27, Kanlıca ☏ 0216 413 9300, ⓦ ajiahotel.com. This is a stunningly beautiful conversion of a splendid nineteenth-century waterfront mansion house, all period charm on the outside and stylish white-is-right minimalism on the inside. The roof-rooms are the best value and have lovely little balconies overlooking the Bosphorus. **€175**

ANASTASIA MEZİKİ MAP P.130. Malül Gazı Cad 24. Ferry from Eminönü or Kadıköy ☏ 0216 383 3444, ⓦ mezikiotel. com. Set in a quiet area of Büyükada's main settlement, this turn-of-the-nineteenth-century villa oozes period charm, with high ceilings, original murals and furniture. You'll really feel like you are stepping back in time here – especially when you have to step out onto the landing at night to use the shared bathrooms. **€44**

MEHTAP 45 MAP P.130. Burgazada. Ferry from Eminönü or Kadıköy ☏ 0216 381 2660. Quiet island, quiet boutique-style hotel with grand views across the Sea of Marmara back to the metropolis. Plain, simple but comfy rooms that were good enough for Bobby Charlton's four-day stay. Note that here, and at most Princes' Island hotels, you pay a fifty percent premium for Saturday-night stays. **€90**

PRENSET PANSİYON MAP P.130. Ayyıldız Cad 40–42/A, Heybeliada. Ferry from Eminönü or Kadıköy ☏ 0216 3051 0039. Cheap and cheerful pension close to the ferry terminal and in the middle of the village close to all the restaurants and cafés. Few rooms have good views. **€45**

SPLENDID PALAS MAP P.130. Nisan Cad 23, Büyükada. Ferry from Eminönü or Kadıköy ☏ 0216 382 6950, ⓦ splendidhotel.net. A grand, white-painted wooden fin de siècle hotel, complete with cupolas and balconies, this period gem once hosted Edward VIII and Mrs Simpson. There's a pool out back and great sea views from the front rooms. Closed Nov–March. **€135**

SUMAHAN ON THE WATER MAP P.128. Kuleli Cad 43, Cengelköy ☏ 0216 422 8000, ⓦ sumahan.com. A distillery converted into an award-winning hotel right on the Asian side of the Bosphorus, in the attractive suburb of Cengelköy. This very stylish place blends the traditional and the modern with verve and makes an ideal retreat from the city hubbub. **€195**

Apartments

DIVAN TAKSIM SUITES MAP P.96, POCKET MAP D10. Cumhüriyet Cad 49 ☏ 0212 254 7777, ⓦ divan.com.tr. Offers some very chic open-plan, Scandinavian-style suites on Taksim Square, complete with work-stations, wi-fi and LCD TVs. **€80**

MEHMET'S PLACE MAP P.74, POCKET MAP B1. Ayvansaray Cad ⓦ airbnb.com. Open-plan, top floor flat with combined kitchen/living room/bedroom area, well located by the Golden Horn waterfront in hip Balat. The best feature is a lovely roof terrace with splendid views of the Horn and Galata, and friendly owner Mehmet, whose mum lives one flat below. **€42**

PASHA MAP P.86, POCKET MAP B14. Serdar-I Ekrem Cad, Galata Tünel İstiklal ⓦ istanbulplace.com. Looking south across the Golden Horn, the sitting room and main bedroom of this beautifully restored nineteenth-century apartment have great old city skyline views. There are three good-sized bedrooms, a stylish kitchen and a separate shower room. Perfect combination of period features and contemporary white decor and furnishings. **€220**

ROOMS GALATA MAP P.86, POCKET MAP B14. Kumbarcı Yokuşu 37 ☏ 0212 293 3186, ⓦ roomsgalata.com. Sixteen cool

Apartments

Apartments are becoming popular in Istanbul, even for short breaks. With some exceptions, they tend to be concentrated in Galata and Beyoğlu and are often part of a converted period townhouse. Good websites include Ⓦ istanbulhubflats.com, with lots of cheaper apartments, and Ⓦ cross-pollinate.com. Below are a few recommended apartments, with prices given for one-night, high-season stays. Note that the government has started to clamp down on companies letting properties without the proper authorisation, so make sure you double-check before you book anything.

rooms in a beautiful period house, linked by a swish spiral staircase. Kitchenettes, wi-fi and king, queen or single beds. **Doubles from €130**

Letting agencies

ARSU LIVING İSTANBUL APARTMENTS Beyoğlu Ⓣ 0531 221 7156, Ⓦ living-istanbul.com. Five reasonably priced apartments either in, or close to, Beyoğlu, run by a German-Turkish couple.

ISTANBUL!PLACE APARTMENTS Galata Ⓣ 0506 449 3393, Ⓦ istanbulplace.com. Anglo-Turkish-run company offering fifteen beautifully restored period townhouse apartments in and around Galata.

MANZARA İSTANBUL Tatarbeyi Sok 26b, Galata Ⓣ 0212 252 4600, Ⓦ manzara-apartments.com. Run by a German-born Turkish architect, this company has forty quality properties, mainly in Galata and Beyoğlu.

ESSENTIALS

Antique tram

Arrival

The vast majority of foreign visitors reach Istanbul by air, though there are good road links and rather less useful rail connections with the rest of Europe. The city is also a major stop on Mediterranean cruises.

By plane

Istanbul has two major airports, Atatürk International (☎ 0212 465 3000, ⊛ ataturkairport.com) on the European side of the city, and Sabiha Gökçen (☎ 0216 585 5000, ⊛ sgairport.com) across the Bosphorus in Asia. The former is used mainly by scheduled airlines; the latter, considerably further from the city centre, by budget European carriers. A third airport is under construction to the north of the city. It is slated to be the world's largest and should be partially operational by 2018. It will eventually replace Atatürk Airport.

New Istanbul airport

Located 54km, about an hour's drive, from the city. All domestic and international flights were supposed to be moved here at the end of 2018, the date keeps being postponed and at the moment of writing, March 3 2019 will mark the beginning of the process. The Atatürk airport will then gradually be closed off to commercial flights, though it will remain open to cargo flights. The construction of the remaining parts of the airport are to be finished by 2028. Buses have been running to the airport since October 29 2018. HAVAIST (⊛ hava.ist) and IETT (⊛ iett.istanbul/en) offer services and the ride takes about 30 to 90 minutes. Travelling to and from Bakırköy costs ₺18 (runs every 10 minutes) and is the same for travelling to and from Yenikapı-Sirkeci (every 11 minutes). In 2020 the M11 metro line to the airport will be opened and a second line is planned for 2022.

Atatürk International airport

Around 24km west of the city centre, this airport comprises two inter-connected terminals, one international, the other domestic. Shuttle buses run by Havabus (⊛ havabus.com) run from both terminals to the city centre every half-hour between 4am and 1am for ₺12. The bus stops near the Marmaray metro terminal at Yenikapı, from where it's one stop to Sirkeci for Eminönü and Sultanahmet. You can also continue to the Havabus terminal at the southern end of Taksim Square for Taksim and Beyoğlu. Journey time is around 30 minutes to Yenikapı, 45 minutes to Taksim, and you pay on the bus. A cheaper alternative is to use a combination of the **M1 Metro** and **T1 tram** (approximately every 10min, 6am–midnight). Follow the "M" signs to the metro and purchase two plastic tokens (jetons) for ₺4 each from the *jetonmatik* machines (see opposite). The metro and tram systems connect at Zeytinburnu; get off here and, using the second jeton, board the T1 tram which will take you to Sultanahmet or across the Golden Horn to Karaköy, where you can take the Tünel funicular (see page 146) to Galata/Beyoğlu or continue to the last stop at Kabataş and take the modern funicular (see page 146) to Taksim Square. It is also possible to buy an Istanbulkart (see box opposite) from a machine at the airport for ₺10, top it up with credit and use that instead of the tokens. Journey time to Sultanahmet should be 30min to 45min. A taxi is around ₺50 to Sultanahmet, ₺60 to Beyoğlu/Taksim.

Sabiha Gökçen airport

Havaş buses (₺15) take around an hour and a half to reach Taksim Square from this airport, departing half-hourly between 4am and 1am. It's also possible to purchase an Istanbulkart

Istanbulkart

This credit card-sized smartcard is available from machines and kiosks near major transport stops. The official price is ₺6 but kiosk vendors usually add a ₺2 mark-up. Bought from a machine the cost is ₺10, which includes ₺4 credit. It can be topped-up when necessary from either a machine or kiosk. Not only does it mean you don't waste time looking for a *jetonmatik* machine, it also saves a substantial ₺1.85 per journey, and much more on Princes' Islands ferries. Another advantage over jetons is that for journeys taken within 1hr 30min of the last the charge is only ₺1.45. It can be used on buses, the metro and tram, ferries and sea buses – plus the suburban train and funiculars.

travel pass (see box) at the airport and thus take a public bus (₺4), the #E10, or #E/11 to Kadıköy, from where you can board a Turyol ferry (6.45am–8.30pm; ₺4) to Eminönü (for Sultanahmet and the old city) or Karaköy (Galata and Beyoğlu). Total journey time will likely be similar to the Havabus. Another choice is the #E/3 bus to Levent and change to the M2 metro to Taksim. A taxi will cost ₺90–110.

By train

Reaching Istanbul by train today is far from the pleasure it must have been in the Orient Express days and is only for the patient and committed rail buff. The most straightforward route from London is via Paris, Munich, Vienna, Budapest and Bucharest. From Bucharest, a train runs to Dimitrovgrad in Bulgaria. Change to the Bosfor Ekspresi, which runs between Sofia and Istanbul, for onward travel to Halkalı, a suburban station some 16km west of central Istanbul. From Halkalı catch the BN1 bus into the city centre, or take a taxi. When work on the Marmaray line (see page 148) is complete, there will be a metro

connection to the city centre. For the best information, see rail enthusiasts' delight ⓦ seat61.com.

By bus

Coaches run by several Turkish companies link Istanbul to other European cities. Ulusoy (ⓦ ulusoy.com. tr) has buses to eleven German cities, while Metro (ⓦ metroturizm.com. tr) runs coaches to Athens, Sofia and Georgia. Buses arrive at Esenler otogar (bus station), linked to the city centre by the M1 metro – switch to the T1 tram at Aksaray. Buses from all Turkish destinations also terminate at Esenler, though some also stop at Harem on the Asian side of the Bosphorus, from where regular ferries cross the strait to Eminönü.

By sea

Cruise ships dock at Karaköy International Maritime Passenger Terminal, on the north side of the Golden Horn not far northeast of the Galata Bridge, from where it's a short walk to the Karaköy T1 tram stop (for Sultanahmet) or the Tünel (for Galata/Beyoğlu).

Getting around

It's fortunate that, despite Istanbul's huge sprawl, most areas of interest are close enough to explore on foot.

Judicious use of the city's metro, tram, bus and ferry network will, however, enable you to get to slightly out of the way places and save your legs. For all of these forms of transport, you use jetons, purchased from the *jetonmatik* machines located at many stops. *Jetonmatik* machines accept Turkish notes and coins and there's a flat-rate charge for most modes of transport of ₺4. The turnstiles at the entrance to tram, metro, train and ferry stops have a slot to accept the jetons. Far superior to jetons is the Istanbulkart travel pass (see page 145).

Buses and dolmuşes

The most daunting of Istanbul's public transport options, as visitors often find it difficult to know which bus to get on or where to get off – plus they can be uncomfortably crowded. Having said that, they are a cheap way of getting around and reaching places other modes of transport (bar taxis) don't. **Municipality buses** are labelled IETT (Istanbul Elektrik Tramway ve Tünel) though there are some private ones. Most run daily 6.30am–11pm. The most useful bus stations in the old city are Beyazıt, Edirnekapı and Eminönü, across the Golden Horn Taksim Square and Kabataş, and there are several routes that may be useful for visitors (see box opposite). **Dolmuşes** are a kind of shared taxi (either a car or minibus) but the only really useful routes are the yellow minibuses departing the Taksim end of Tarlabaşı Bulvarı for the old city and Yedikule (see page 79) or connecting Kadıköy and Üsküdar in Asia. Note that you need cash.

Trams

The most useful transport route for visitors is the T1 tramline, which runs from Zeytinburnu in the west (where it connects with the M1 metro and thus Atatürk airport) to the ferry terminal/bus station and funicular at Kabataş, on the north side of the Golden Horn. It heads through the old city, with stops including the Grand Bazaar,

Sultanahmet, Sirkeci, Eminönü (for ferries to Asia), Karaköy (for ferries to Asia and Galata and the Tünel to Beyoğlu) and Kabataş (for the funicular to Taksim and buses along the European shore of the Bosphorus). Note that Kabataş ferry terminal is closed indefinitely. The so-called **antique tram** (daily 9am–9pm; ₺4) rumbles up and down İstiklal Caddesi from Tünel İstiklal to Taksim Square.

Metro

There are several lines but only the M1, M2 and Marmaray lines will be of use to the majority of visitors. The M1 metro links Atatürk airport with Esenler bus station and Aksaray – though doesn't link up perfectly with the T1 tram at Aksaray and you have to walk 200m over a bridge to swap from the Aksaray M1 metro stop to the T1 tram stop at Yusufpaşa. A better option is to change from the M1 metro to the T1 tram at Zeytinburnu. The M1 metro is useful for getting out to the land walls reasonably close to the Kariye Museum (see page 72). The M2 metro runs from Yenikapı in the old city north across the Golden Horn to Şişhane at the southern end of İstiklal Caddesi. From there, it runs north again to Taksim and out to the suburbs. At the time of writing, the Marmaray line was running between Kazlıçeşme in the west (useful for the southern terminus of the land walls of Theodosius) eastwards to Yenikapı (where it connects with the M2 metro) then to Sirkeci, under the Bosphorus to Üsküdar and on to Ayrılık Çeşmesi, where it connects to the M4 metro for Kadıköy. Eventually it will be extended to Halkalı in the west, Gebze to the east.

Funiculars

The F1 funicular links the transport hub at Kabataş with Taksim Square, while the nineteenth-century

Useful bus routes

For information in English on the bus network in Istanbul, check Ⓦ iett.istanbul/en. It's tricky to use – on the home page click on the route planner for details of routes, stops and maps.

Istanbul in Asia

#12 and **#12/A** Kadıköy to Üsküdar

#15 Üsküdar along the Bosphorus to Beylerbeyi, Kanlıca and Beykoz

#15/A Beykoz to Anadolu Kavağı

European Istanbul

#22 Kabataş along the Bosphorus to İstiniye via Beşiktaş, Ortaköy, Arnavutköy, Bebek and Emirgan

#25/A Haciosman metro to Rumeli Kavağı via Tarabya and Sariyer

#25/E Kabataş to Sariyer via Beşiktaş, Ortaköy, Arnavutköy, Bebek and Emirgan

#28 Beşiktaş to Edirnekapı via Eminönü Transit and Fatih (for Fatih and Yavuz Selim mosques, land walls and Kariye Museum)

#28/T Beşiktaş to Topkapı via Karaköy, Eminönü Transit and Fatih

#36/V and **#37/Y** Vezneciler to Edirnekapı via Fatih (for Fatih and Yavuz Selim mosques, land walls and Kariye Museum)

#38/E Eminönü to Edirnekapı via Unkapanı Bridge and Fatih (for Fatih and Yavuz Selim mosques, land walls and Kariye Museum)

#38 Beyazıt to Edirnekapı via Aksaray (for Historia Mall, Akdeniz Hatay Sofrası, land walls, Kariye Museum)

#40 Taksim to Sariyer via Beşiktaş, Ortaköy, Arnavutköy, Bebek and Emirgan

#55/EB Beyazıt to Eyüp via Aksaray, Fatih and Edirnekapı (for Yavuz Selim mosque, land walls, Kariye Museum and *Pierre Loti* café)

#54/HT Taksim to upper Golden Horn (for Miniatürk, Rahmi M. Koç Industrial Museum and Santralistanbul)

#80/T Taksim to Yedikule (for south end of land walls)

#87 Taksim to Edirnekapı via Fatih (for Fatih and Yavuz Selim mosques, land walls and Kariye Museum)

#99 Eminönü along Golden Horn (for Fener, Balat, north end of land walls, Eyüp and Santralistanbul)

or Istanbulkart), connects Karaköy on the Golden Horn with Beyoğlu/İstiklal Caddesi at the top of the hill. There's also a **cable car** (t4 or Istanbulkart) linking the shores of the Golden Horn at Eyüp with the cemetery and *Pierre Loti* café (see page 82).

Ferries

Few will want to visit Istanbul and not take a ferry ride to Asia and/or up the Bosphorus or Golden Horn. Şehir Hatları (Ⓣ 0212 313 8000, Ⓦ sehirhatlari.istanbul) is the main company – make sure you pick up a timetable from a ferry terminal or tourist office as times do change, or check their website. The main city terminal is at Eminönü, just east of the Galata Bridge, from where ferries run across the Bosphorus to Kadıköy (Mon–Fri 7.30am–9pm, Sat & Sun 7.40am–9pm; t4) and Üsküdar (Mon–Sat 6.50am–10.30pm, Sun 7.30am–10.30pm; t4) around three to five times an hour (they are primarily for commuters). The terminal for the Şehir Hatları Bosphorus Cruise (see page 126) is also here. To the west of the bridge, from Yemiş İskele, Haliç Hattı ferries originating from Üsküdar run (approximately hourly) up the Golden Horn to Eyüp, which is useful for visits to the Rahmi M. Koç Industrial Museum (see page 88), the northern end of the land walls. From Karaköy, across the Galata Bridge, there are ferries to Kadıköy (6.30am–midnight; t3). Until the completion of the new ferry terminal at Kabataş, postponed but allegedly not stopped, ferries to the Princes' Islands run mainly from Eminönü, stopping at Kadıköy. On completion, Princes' Islands ferries and faster Istanbul Deniz Otobüslersea buses (ido.com.tr) will likely return to Kabataş – more details can be found in Chapter 9 (see page 131). A number of smaller private companies also operate boats across the Bosphorus and to the Princes' Islands, notably Turyol, with boats departing to Asia from terminals just west of the Galata Bridge on both sides of the Golden Horn.

Taxis

Yellow taxis are ubiquitous and are very useful when visiting out-of-the-way sights and, assuming the driver is honest, reasonably cheap (a standing charge of t3.5, then t2.1 per km). Make sure the meter is turned on before setting off – ensuring the driver follows the shortest route is trickier. One way to avoid potential disputes is to get your hotel to arrange a taxi for you for an agreed price.

Tourist buses

Big Bus Istanbul (☎ 0212 283 1396, ⓦ bigbustours.com) has a hop-on, hop-off service with a recorded guide. Departures are from either opposite the Haghia Sophia or across the Golden Horn in Taksim, where there are red kiosks selling tour tickets. There are two routes: the Blue Route covers the old city and the north side of the Golden Horn; the Red Route crosses the Golden Horn and the Bosphorus to Asia. A combined ticket is €30.

Walking and special interest tours

Istanbul Walks (☎ 0216 335 662, ⓦ istanbulwalks.com) offers guided walks of the city that include all the major historic sites (admission not included) for around €70 for a full day. More specialist is Fest Travel (☎ 0850 622 3378, ⓦ festtravel.com), with a wide range of strolls around quarters of the city where it's easy to miss the most interesting sights if you are on your own. Istanbul Tour Studio (☎ 0212 243 0521, ⓦ istanbultourstudio.com) offer a range of activities including sailing, rowing on the Golden Horn, cycling in Asia and exploring the city's street art scene.

Transport infrastructure projects

The Marmaray transport infrastructure project includes a rail tunnel under the Bosphorus linking European and Asian Istanbul. The tunnel finally opened in 2013 after years of delays caused by the uncovering of archeological finds while digging the Yenikapı hub. From Yenikapı, the line runs to Sirkeci, then to Üsküdar and west to Kazlıçeşme. In 2014 the construction of a controversial bridge across the Golden Horn allowed the M2 to link with the Marmaray line. The Yavuz Sultan Selim Bridge, a third one across the Bosphorus carrying road and rail traffic, opened in 2016. Late the same year a new road tunnel opened under the river, linking Kazlıçeşme in Europe with Harem in Asia. In 2019 the construction of the Canal Istanbul is set to begin.

Directory A–Z

Cinema

Most films are screened in the language in which they were shot, with Turkish subtitles for non-Turkish productions. The exceptions are children's films, which are generally dubbed into Turkish. There are several cinemas on or just off İstiklal Caddesi between Galatasaray Meydanı and Taksim Square (see page 100), the largest of which is Cinemaximum Fitaş (ⓦintersinema.com), and there's one in Sultanahmet, the Şafak (ⓦozenfilm. com.tr). Otherwise, head to one of the big shopping malls. Tickets from t10.

Consulates

Australia Asker Ocağı Cad 15, Elmadağ, Şişli ⓣ0212 393 8542.
Canada Tekfen Tower, 209 Büyükdere Cad, Levent 4 ⓣ0212 272 5174.
New Zealand İnönü Cad 48/3, Taksim ⓣ0212 244 0272.
South Africa (Honorary Consul) Alarko Centre, Muallim Naci Cad 113–115, Ortaköy ⓣ0212 260 378.
UK Meşrutiyet Cad 34, Tepebaşı, Beyoğlu ⓣ0212 334 6400.
US Kaplıcalar Mevkii Sok 2, İstinye ⓣ0212 335 9000.

Crime

Mugging and assaults are rare, though pickpocketing is increasingly common – take care on the crowded transport system. Be wary of Taksim Square at night, notably where it joins Tarlabaşı Bulvarı, and the land walls at dusk/evening time. There are several police forces in Turkey but the branch you're most likely to require is the Security Police (Emniyet Polisi), recognized by their blue shirts. The Tourist Police (Turizm Polisi) have a station, open 24hr, at Yerebatan Cad 6 (ⓣ0212 527 4503). Blue-uniformed Market Police (Zabitas) patrol commercial areas.

Electricity

220V AC. Plugs have two round pins so bring an adaptor if necessary.

Entry requirements

Make sure you have a full passport with at least six months' validity. Citizens of most countries must buy an e-visa in advance from ⓦevisa. gov.tr. Visas are multiple entry and for citizens of the UK, Ireland, the US, Canada, Australia and New Zealand, are valid for 90 days in 180 days from the date requested on the application. Visas for citizens of the UK, USA and Ireland are $20, Australia and Canada $60. Note that entry requirements change; consult the Turkish Ministry of Foreign Affairs at ⓦmfa.gov.tr for the latest regulations.

Health

For minor complaints visit a pharmacy (*eczane*). Many pharmacists speak English and most antibiotics are available without a prescription. Pharmacies open 9am–7pm Mon–Sat but there is always a night duty pharmacy (*nöbetçi eczane*) open 24hr including Sundays – the address of the nearest is posted in pharmacy windows.

Both public and private hospitals are well equipped, but state hospitals are often overcrowded and run-down. Private establishments usually have more English-speaking doctors and often a designated translator. Facilities are generally top-notch and they are well-used to dealing with foreign private patients (and relieving them of their cash – make sure you're insured).

The Taksim First Aid Hospital (Taksim İlkyardim Hastanesi) at Sıraselviler Cad 112, Taksim (ⓣ0212 252 4300), is state-run and only treats emergencies. The private American

Emergency numbers

Ambulance ☎ 112
Fire ☎ 110
Police ☎ 155
Traffic Police ☎ 154

Hospital (Amerikan Hastanesi), Güzelbahçe Sok 20, Nişantaşı (☎ 0212 311 2000, �W amerikanhastanesi. org), is state-of-the-art and also has a dental clinic. The International Hospital, İstanbul Cad 82, Yeşilköy (☎ 0212 468 4444, �W www. internationalhospital.com.tr), has a full range of medical services and 24hr emergency care. For a regular rather than hospital dentist, Prodent (Can Ergene) at Valikonağı Cad 109/5, Nişantaşı (☎ 0212 230 4635), is reliable and English-speaking. Dental care is generally both excellent and relatively cheap in Turkey.

Internet

Virtually every hostel, pension and hotel in Istanbul offers free wi-fi and often a fixed terminal or two as well. Many upmarket cafés also have free wi-fi, especially those situated in Galata and Beyoğlu. There are also plenty of internet cafés, though many of these are mainly frequented by youths gaming.

Left luggage

There are lockers at both Atatürk and Sabiha Gökçen airports (₺18 for 24hr).

LGBTQ travellers

Istanbul has a very active LGBTQ scene despite the ambivalence of Turkish society to homosexuality. The scene is centred largely on Taksim and Beyoğlu, where there are a number of LGBTQ cafés and clubs. For more information see ⊕ istanbulgay.com or, for LGBTQ-friendly accommodation, check ⊕ gayhomestays.com/top-destinations/Istanbul/.

Lost property

For anything lost (or stolen) contact the Tourist Police at Yerebatan Cad 6 (☎ 0212 527 4503) in Sultanahmet.

Money

Turkey's currency is the Turkish lira (*Türk lirası*) or TL for short, divided into smaller units known as kuruş. Coins come in denominations of 1, 5, 10, 25, 50 kuruş and 1TL, with notes in denominations of 5, 10, 20, 50, 100 and 200TL. Prices of goods and services are displayed as either 25TL, for example, or using the symbol ₺. At the time of writing, the ₺ symbol was being used by businesses either in front of the numerical figure or after it; officially it should be placed before.

There are many, many ATMs throughout the city. All have touch-screen English options, those in major tourist areas dispense euros and dollars as well as Turkish lira. Many banks will change money but they can be slow and cumbersome – for the best rate use the state-owned Ziraat Bankası (Mon–Fri 8.30am–noon & 1.30pm–5pm), which has a dedicated exchange counter and an automated queuing system. You can also change money at the Post Office (PTT) commission-free and at a reasonable rate. The other alternative is an exchange bureau (döviz bürosu). The rate is usually slightly less than the Ziraat Bankası but the procedure much quicker, and opening hours are longer (generally Mon–Sat 9am–8pm) than banks'. There are several around the Sultanahmet tram-stop area on Divan Yolu as well as on İstiklal Caddesi. Credit cards are widely accepted in most tourist-orientated hotels and upmarket restaurants but sometimes attract a surcharge.

Mosque essentials

Turkey is ninety-nine percent Muslim, and although Istanbul is a vibrant, cosmopolitan city, many of its inhabitants take their religion seriously so it pays to be respectful when visiting mosques. The basic rules of entry are:

Cover your head (women) and shoulders and upper arms (men and women).

No shorts (either sex) or miniskirts

Take off shoes before entering (often a plastic bag is provided for you to place your shoes in and carry around; alternatively, place them on one of the shelves provided).

Friday midday prayers are the most important of the week and visiting at this time is not advised – indeed, visiting at any of the five daily prayer times is best avoided, though in most cases you will not cause offence. Don't speak too loudly (there are often people in the mosque either praying or learning the Koran) and don't point your camera at worshippers. Mosques always have a donation box which you may want to contribute to. Take note that there are no set opening and closing times and many of the big mosques in the old city will be open all day, from first to last prayer call (which varies through the year according to sunrise and sunset). Smaller mosques in more out of the way places are often kept locked outside prayer times and you may need to track down the caretaker or imam.

Museum passes

Five-day Istanbul Museum passes can be both cost and time effective. The pass (₺85) gives entry to Haghia Sophia, Haghia Eirene, the Kariye Museum, Galata Mevlevî Lodge, the Fethiye Museum, the Topkapı Palace and Harem, the Archeology Museum, the Mosaic Museum, and the Museum of Turkish and Islamic Art and History of Science and Technology in Islam Museum, a substantial saving on individual entries. The pass allows fast-track entry to sites – useful as Haghia Sophia and Topkapı often have interminable queues. Possession of the pass also gives discounted entry to several other museums in the city. Passes are available from the first four museums listed above or online from Ⓦ muze.gov.tr.

Opening hours

Although in Turkey state-run museums invariably close on a Monday, some in Istanbul buck this rule, so make sure you check the opening days of a particular museum before visiting. Opening hours are often April–Oct 9am–7pm and Nov–March 9am–5pm, but some have the same opening hours year round so check before visiting.

Security threats

Due in no small part to fear over terrorist attacks, Turkey suffered an over thirty-percent drop in visitor numbers in 2016, with Istanbul faring even worse. The threat should not be taken lightly: there were several high-profile attacks in 2016, and in the early hours of 2017 a gunman killed 39 at *Reina* nightclub. Airport-style security has been introduced at major tourist attractions in Istanbul, and safety measures have been tightened city-wide. Stay well away from demonstrations and be sure to consult the latest government travel advice ahead of time, and you're likely to enjoy a safe visit.

For mosques see "Mosque essentials". Private museums follow the same general opening hours as their state-run cousins but sometimes shut for lunch. Banks and government offices usually open Mon–Fri 8.30am–noon and 1.30–5pm. Shop opening hours vary widely, with most opening from between 9am or 10am–7pm, but many more, especially in Beyoğlu, stay open until 9 or 10pm. *Bakkals*, small general stores, and kiosks selling papers, gum, tissues etc are often open from 7am–10pm. The Grand Bazaar is open Mon–Sat 9am–7pm, modern malls usually 10am–10pm seven days a week.

Phones

Note that Istanbul has two codes, 0212 for the European side of the city, 0216 for the Asian. Turkey's country code is 90, directory enquiries 118 and 115 for the international operator. To phone overseas, purchase an international calling card, the best of which is the Alocard, available from PTTs and usable at public phones – just dial the access number supplied with the card, scratch to reveal the 12-digit PIN and enter it, then dial the overseas number. A ₺10 card allows over 1hr 15min of calling time to the UK or US. There are plenty of public phone booths scattered around the city, often outside major transport hubs such as Sirkeci, and also at PTTs. Assuming you have a roaming facility your mobile will connect with one of the local providers, though US phones won't work here. Calls are predictably expensive, around £1.30 per minute to the UK, plus you pay for incoming calls. Unfortunately, buying a cheap SIM card is not a great option here as legislation is strict and taxes high. The three main providers (Türkcell, AVEA and Vodaphone) have outlets at both Atatürk and Sabiha Gökçen airports where you must complete a registration form and have your passport photocopied. A typical pay-as-you-go package is ₺120, only ₺70 of which is credit, the rest tax. After 120 days your phone will be blocked for use with the Turkish SIM unless you pay a ₺150 fee at a local tax office.

Post

The two main post offices (PTT) are the massive Sirkeci PTT on Büyük Postane Caddesi, Eminönü (daily 8.30am–7pm; ☎ 0212 526 1200), and at Yeniçarşısı Caddesi, Beyoğlu (Mon–Fri & Sun 8.30am–5.30pm; ☎ 0212 444 1788), just off Galatasaray Meydanı.

Smoking

Smoking is banned on public transport and in all indoor places, although the ban is widely flouted in some bars and traditional teahouses. Many bars, cafés and restaurants get around the ban by providing outside or courtyard tables, which are covered with plastic and/or warmed with heaters in winter. The rule applies to *nargile* (water pipe) cafés.

Time

Turkey is two hours ahead of GMT in summer, and three in winter. There is no am/pm in Turkey, which uses the 24-hour clock.

Tipping

A ten to fifteen percent service charge is standard in fancy restaurants, though as this goes to the establishment, you should tip the waiters a further five. Waiters in basic establishments will also appreciate the same.

Toilets

In heavily touristed parts of the city there are sufficient public toilets, in less-visited parts like the land walls and northwest quarter far fewer. Virtually all mosques have toilets attached. At both public and mosque toilets you have to pay a small fee (usually ₺1) and note that they are invariably of the squat variety and provide no paper. Bars, cafés, restaurants and hotels all have western-style toilets.

Tourist information

There are six tourist offices. Most central is at Divan Yolu 3, Sultanahmet (daily 9am–5pm; ☏ 0212 518 8754) near the Haghia Sophia, which has English-speaking staff and maps. The other old city offices at Beyazıt Meydanı (daily 9am–6pm; ☏ 0212 522 4902) near the Grand Bazaar, and at Sirkeci station (daily 9am–5pm; ☏ 0212 511 5888) are less helpful. In Taksim, there's one in the Hilton, Cumhüriyet Caddesi (daily 9am–5pm; ☏ 0212 518 8754), for cruise ship arrivals, on Kemaneş Caddesi, Karaköy (daily 9am–5pm; ☏ 0212 249 5776).

Travellers with disabilities

The good news is that the useful T1 tram is reasonably disabled-friendly and will save time and effort pushing a wheelchair along busy Divan Yolu. The metro has few accessible stations. Buses have ramps and low doors, but are so crowded that using them is tricky, especially given the language barrier, and they are not allowed into Sultanahmet. The Topkapı Palace (see page 43), Haghia Sophia (see page 25) and Archeology Museum (see page 42) are partly accessible by wheelchair, as is the Blue Mosque (see page 34). Unfortunately, the old city's steep streets and cobbled surfaces can make it difficult to get around between sights, and few mosques allow wheelchairs. Despite friendly and helpful staff, many other museums and sights do not have wheelchair access, with the honourable exceptions of the Rahmi M. Koç Industrial Museum (see page 88), Istanbul Modern (see page 94) and the Pera Museum (see page 98).

Travelling with children

While there are few specifically child-friendly sights in Istanbul, and it can appear dauntingly crowded and hectic at times, most kids will find Istanbul an absorbing place to visit. The boat rides up and down the Bosphorus, across to Asia and out to the Princes' Islands are all great fun with kids, and several of the city's museums and galleries will be of interest. The Military Museum (see page 101) may be a little stuffy but has enough weaponry to keep kids of a certain age quiet for a while, as will the detailed scale models in Miniatürk (see page 89). Then there are the hands-on science machines at Santralistanbul (see page 89) and the plethora of vintage modes of transport and more at the Rahmi Koç Industrial Museum – plus the life-like panorama of the 1453 siege of Constantinople at the Panorama 1453 Museum (see page 80). Both Gülhane Park (see page 49) and Yıldız Park (see page 115) have plenty of green and open space for kids to run off some energy. Turks love kids, the family means everything here and cafés and restaurants are usually very tolerant of them.

Turkish baths (hamam)

Essentially a continuation of the Roman tradition, the Ottoman Turks made the hamam a central feature of everyday life and they were often attached to the great imperial mosque complexes such as the Süleymaniye (see page 58). Today the importance of the hamam has declined significantly, though they are still used by locals to relax and meet up with friends. For many visitors the hamam experience is a must, especially in Istanbul as it boasts many historic hamams, worth seeing for their architecture alone. Some have separate sections for men and women, others are segregated according to a schedule. The vast majority have a foyer/changing area, often with a café, and somewhere to leave your valuables. The main event is the steamy, domed *hararet*, where bathers soap-up and sluice themselves with water of varying degrees of hot and cold, or lie on the *göbek taşı* or navel stone, a raised and heated marble platform in the centre of the room. There is a basic charge for this self-service bath, the traditional scrub and massage are extra. Detailed information on seven hamams is given in the relevant Places chapters; in the old city the Ayasofya Hürrem Sultan (see page 30), Cağaloğlu (see page 49), Çemberlitaş (see page 63) and Süleymaniye (see page 59); Tophane the Kılıç Ali Paşa (see page 88), in Beyoğlu the Galatasaray Hamamı (see page 99); and in Üsküdar the Çinili (see page 118).

Festivals and events

Public holidays are denoted by PH and banks, schools and government offices close on these days, though most private businesses, including cafés and restaurants, stay open, and all transport runs as normal. Tickets for many events can be bought online from ⓦ biletix.com and ⓦ pozitif.com. For more information visit ⓦ iksv.org/eng or ask in one of the city tourist offices.

NEW YEAR'S DAY (PH)

January 1

ISTANBUL FILM FESTIVAL

April ⓦ film.iksv.org/en
Twelve-day film festival featuring a decent mix of domestic and foreign flicks. This is a good chance to see some of the best new Turkish films with English subtitles.

TULIP FESTIVAL

Mid-April to mid-May
Over fifteen million tulip bulbs planted across the city bloom at this time, and there are plenty of associated celebrations. The most convenient places to see Turkey's national flower are Gülhane, Yıldız and Emirgan parks.

CHILDREN'S DAY (PH)

April 23
A celebration of Turkish independence and Turkey's children, school-band marches take place across the city, notably on İstiklal Caddesi.

YOUTH AND SPORTS DAY (PH)

May 19
Marches and celebrations on the anniversary of the day Atatürk launched the Turkish War of Independence.

INTERNATIONAL THEATRE FESTIVAL

Mid-May to early June ⓦ iksv.org/en
Major festival featuring Turkish and foreign theatre companies performing in venues such as the Rumeli Hisarı fortress on the Bosphorus.

CHILL-OUT

May ⓦ chilloutfest.com
One-day dance, electronic and pop festival held at Life Park.

CONQUEST CELEBRATIONS

May 29 ⓦ ibb.gov.tr
Week-long festivities around the anniversary of the fall of Constantinople to the Ottoman Turks, with concerts by the military Mehter Band, parades and fireworks.

SHOPPING FESTIVAL

July ⓦ istshopfest.com
Ninety or so shopping centres stay open 24hr a day, new fashions go on show and there are big discounts at various locations around the city, as well as a number of special events.

ISTANBUL MUSIC FESTIVAL

Mid–June to mid–July Ⓦ iksv.org/en
Lasting most of the month, concerts, dance and opera are performed at some interesting venues by a mix of Turkish and international performers.

EFES PILSEN ONE LOVE

Last weekend June or early July
Ⓦ www.fespilsenonelove.com
Weekend-long indie music festival usually held in Parkorman.

ISTANBUL JAZZ FESTIVAL

First two weeks of July Ⓦ iksv.org/en
Music – not all of it is jazz – played at a series of venues across the city.

VICTORY DAY (PH)

August 30
Celebrates the victory of the Turks over the invading Greeks at the Battle of Dumlupınar in 1922.

CONTEMPORARY ISTANBUL

September Ⓦ contemporaryistanbul.com
This is a major, week-long arts fair based in the prestigious Lütfi Kırdar Congress and Exhibition Centre.

INTERNATIONAL ISTANBUL BIENNIAL

Mid–September to mid–November
Ⓦ iksv.org/en
Held odd years in venues across the city, this is a major contemporary arts event.

REPUBLIC DAY (PH)

October 29
Street parade by schoolchildren to mark the foundation of the Turkish Republic on this day in 1923.

AKBANK INTERNATIONAL JAZZ FESTIVAL

First three weeks in November
Ⓦ akbanksanat.com

Religious holidays

The religious festivals observed throughout the Islamic world also apply to Istanbul. **Ramazan** (Ramadan), the period of fasting for the month preceding **Şeker Bayramı** (Eid ul Fitr in Arabic) is not a holiday, but if your visit coincides with this month you may notice that some cafés and restaurants, especially away from the tourist haunts, are unusually quiet in the day, and packed with fast-breakers after sunset. Try to avoid eating and drinking too obviously in front of people in conservative areas like Fatih (northwest quarter). Şeker Bayramı is usually a three-day festival and banks, government offices and many private businesses are closed for the entire period, though transport continues to run. Museums are usually shut only on the first day of the holiday. **Kurban Bayramı** (Eid ul Adha in Arabic) is a four-day festival during which animals are slaughtered to commemorate Abraham sacrificing a ram instead of his son. The same rules regarding closures apply as for Şeker Bayramı. As the Muslim calendar is lunar, the festivals occur eleven days earlier each year.

Şeker Bayramı	Kurban Bayramı
2019 Şeker June 5–7	Kurban Aug 11–14
2020 Şeker May 24–26	Kurban July 31–Aug 3
2021 Şeker May 12–14	Kurban July 20–23
2022 Şeker May 1–3	Kurban July 8–11

Quality jazz festival with leading domestic and foreign artists performing at venues such as Babylon, İKSV Salon and the Lütfi Kırdar Congress Centre.

ATATÜRK'S DEATH (PH)

November 10
The founder of the Republic died at the Dolmabahçe Palace on this day in 1938. At 9.05am, the time of his death, people throughout the city and country stop what they are doing and observe a five-minute silence.

ISTANBUL SHORT FILM FESTIVAL

Mid-December ⓦ istanbulfilmfestival.com
During this festival over a thousand short films from Turkey and around the world are screened in cinemas across the city.

Chronology

c.6500 BC Neolithic human settlement on the site of Istanbul.

c.667 BC The legendary foundation of Byzantium (Istanbul) by Greek colonists led by Byzas.

513 BC Darius, King of Persia, captures Byzantium.

334 BC Alexander the Great captures Byzantium.

195 AD Roman emperor Septimius Severus burns the city down, rebuilds it a few years later.

324 AD Emperor Constantine decides the city will be his new imperial capital, building starts.

330 Constantine calls the rebuilt city Nova Roma, but it's soon known as Constantinople.

337 Constantine is baptized a Christian.

392 Paganism is banned by Emperor Theodosius and the Roman Empire becomes overtly Christian.

447 The land walls are rebuilt following a massive earthquake.

532 The Nika riots cause vast damage to the city before 30,000 of the rioters are massacred in the Hippodrome.

537 A monumental new cathedral, the Haghia Sophia (Aya Sofya) is completed on the site of an earlier incarnation burned in the 532 riots.

674 The Arabs besiege Constantinople; the defenders use "Greek fire" against their enemy.

726 Emperor Leo III forbids icon veneration as idolatry, causing riots across the empire.

1054 Schism of the Orthodox and Catholic churches.

1071 The first Turks reach Anatolia and defeat Emperor Romanos IV Diogenes at Manzikert.

1097 The First Crusade passes through Constantinople.

1204 The Fourth Crusade captures Constantinople and irrevocably weakens the Byzantine Empire.

1261 Michael VIII Palaeologus recaptures the city for the Byzantines.

1326 The Osmanlı (Ottomans to the West), a Turkish tribal group, capture Bursa and further weaken the Byzantine Empire.

1453 The Ottomans capture Constantinople on May 29 after a two-month siege. The Byzantine Empire is extinguished.

1459 Construction of the Topkapı Palace, the heart of the Ottoman Empire, begins.

1481 Beyazıt II becomes Sultan.

1492 Beyazıt II sends an Ottoman fleet to Spain to save the Jews from persecution.

1514 Selim I "the Grim" wins a crucial victory over the Persians.

1517 Selim I captures Medina, takes the title of Caliph.

1529 The Ottomans reach the gates of Vienna led by Süleyman the Magnificent.

1558 The completion of the Süleymaniye Camii by Sinan.

1571 Don John of Austria defeats the Ottoman navy at Lepanto.

1616 The monumental Sultanahmet Camii is completed after eight years' toil.

1729 Sultan Ahmet I establishes the Ottoman Empire's first printing press.

1779 The Ottomans lose the Crimea to Russia.

1830 Greece fights off Ottoman control and becomes an independent state.

1839 Sultan Abdülmecid begins to reform the empire on European lines.

1853 Tsar Nicholas I of Russia declares the Ottoman Empire the "sick man of Europe".

1854 Florence Nightingale arrives.

1856 Abdülmecit leaves Topkapı Palace and moves to European-style Dolmabahçe Palace.

1888 Visitors from Europe reach Istanbul on the new Orient Express.

1889 Foundation of The Committee for Union and Progress (CUP) or Young Turks as they are better known.

1909 Sultan Abdülhamit deposed by the CUP.

1914 Ottoman Turkey signs an alliance with Germany and enters World War I.

1918 Britain occupies Istanbul after the Allied victory in World War I.

1919 Mustafa Kemal lands at Samsun on the Black Sea, triggering the Turkish War of Independence.

1922 The Sultanate is abolished by Turkish nationalists led by Atatürk.

1923 The Republic of Turkey is officially founded, Ankara replaces Istanbul as capital.

1934 Haghia Sophia (Aya Sofya), a church then a mosque, becomes a museum.

1938 Atatürk dies at Dolmabahçe Palace.

1939 Turkey remains neutral for most of World War II, Istanbul a centre of intrigue.

1955 A weekend of rioting destroys many Greek minority-owned properties on İstiklal Caddesi and across the city.

1960 Turkey's first military coup.

1971 Second military coup.

1923 The Republic of Turkey is officially founded, Ankara replaces Istanbul as capital.

1934 Haghia Sophia (Aya Sofya), a church then a mosque, becomes a museum.

1938 Atatürk dies at Dolmabahçe Palace.

1939 Turkey remains neutral for most of World War II, Istanbul a centre of intrigue.

1955 A weekend of rioting destroys many Greek minority-owned properties on İstiklal Caddesi and across the city.

1960 Turkey's first military coup.

1971 Second military coup.

1977 Thirty-nine leftist demonstrators shot by extremists at a May Day rally in Taksim Square.

1980 Turkey's third military coup.

1994 A pro-Islamic Refah Party wins Istanbul in municipal elections, Tayyip Erdoğan becomes mayor.

2002 Pro-Islamic AKP sweep to power in general elections led by Tayyip Erdoğan.

2010 Istanbul is joint European Capital of Culture.

2011 The AKP wins the general elections for a record third time.

2013 Protests erupt in Gezi Park when the government tries to replace a green area with a shopping mall.

2014 Tayyip Erdoğan becomes Turkey's first popularly elected president.

2015 The AKP win the general elections for the fourth time.

2016 A series of terrorist attacks in Istanbul cast a shadow over the country.

2018 New Istanbul Airport opens.

2019 Beginning of the Canal Istanbul construction.

Turkish

Few visitors to Istanbul speak any Turkish and only a handful bother to try to learn any. This is a great shame as a very little Turkish can go a long way not only in helping you negotiate your way around the city – particularly its less visited quarters – but also in showing that you have an interest in an intensely proud people who often feel that they are misunderstood by foreigners. Below is a brief guide to pronunciation, some useful words and phrases and a basic glossary for food and drink. For a more comprehensive introduction, see *The Rough Guide Turkish Phrasebook*.

Pronunciation

Turkish is phonetically spelt and, compared to most other languages, grammatically regular. It is lightly stressed, usually on the last syllable. It uses the following letters which do not appear in the English version of the Latin alphabet – ç, ğ, ı, ö, ş, ü – but does not contain the letters q, w or x. Below is a brief pronunciation guide.

Aa short a, as in car
Ee as in pet
İi as in bin
Iı an uh sound
Oo as in dote

Öö like **ur** in ch**ur**n
Uu as in cl**ue**
Üü like **ew** in d**ew**
Cc like **j** in **j**elly
Çç like **ch** in **ch**ang
Gg like **g** as in **g**o
Ğğ hardly pronounced, but slightly lengthens the preceding vowel
Hh as in **h**ate
Jj like the **s** in trea**s**ure
Şş like **sh** in **sh**op
Vv between a **v** and a **w**

Words and phrases

BASICS

good morning günaydın
good afternoon iyi günler
good evening iyi akşamlar
good night iyi geceler
hello merhaba
goodbye Allaha ısmarladık
yes evet
no hayır
no (there isn't/aren't any) yok
please lütfen
thank you teşekkür ederim/ sağol
you're welcome bir şey değil
How are you? Nasılsınız? Nasılsın?
I'm fine İyiyim
Do you speak English? İngilizce biliyormusunuz?
I don't know bilmiyorum
I beg your pardon affedersiniz
excuse me pardon
I'm English/ İngilizim/ **Scottish/** İskoçyalım/ **Irish/** İrlandalıyım/ **American/** Amerikalı/ **Australian/** Avustralyalım
today bugün
tomorrow yarın
yesterday dün
now şimdi
later sonra
in the morning sabahleyin
in the afternoon oğle'den sonra
in the evening akşamleyin
here/there/over there bur(a)da/şur(a)da/ or(a) da
good/bad iyi/kötü, fena
big/small büyük/küçük

cheap/expensive ucuz/pahalı
early/late erken/geç
hot/cold sıcak/soğuk
near/far yakın/uzak
vacant/occupied boş/dolu
Mr Bey (follows first name)
Miss Bayan (precedes first name)
Mrs Hanım (follows first name)

QUESTIONS AND DIRECTIONS

Where is the...? ...Nerede?
When? Ne zaman?
What/What is it? Ne/ne dir?
How much (does it cost?) Ne kadar/kaç para?
How many? Kaç tane?
What time is it? Saat kaç?
How do I get to...? ...'a/e nasıl giderim?
How far is it to...? ...'a/e ne kadar uzak?
When does it open? Saat kaçta açılıyor?
When does it close? Saat kaçta kapanıyor?

TRANSPORT

aeroplane uçak
bus otobüs
train tren
car araba
taxi taksi
ferry feribot, vapur
catamaran, sea bus deniz otobüsü
bus station otogar
railway station gar, tren ıstasyonu
ferry terminal/jetty iskele
A ticket to... ...'a bir bilet
one-way gidiş sadece
return gidiş-dönüş
What time does it leave? Saat kaçta kalkıyor?
Where does it leave from? Nereden kalkıyor?

SIGNS

açık/kapalı open/closed
baylar gentlemen
bayanlar ladies
çekiniz/itiniz pull/push
dikkat beware
dur stop, halt
giriş/çıkış entrance/exit
girmek yasaktır entry forbidden

ilk yardım first aid
lütfen ayakkabılarınızı çıkartınız please take off your shoes
sigara içilmez no smoking
WC/tuvalet WC

ACCOMMODATION

hotel otel
pension pansiyon
Do you have a room? Boş odanız var mı?
single/double/triple Tek/çift/üç kişilik
with a double bed fransız yataklı
with a shower duşlu
hot water sıcak su
cold water soğuk su
Can I see it? Bakabilirmiyim?
I have a booking Reservasyonum var
Is there wi-fi? Kablosuz internet var mı?
What's the password? Şifre nedir?

NUMBERS

bir 1
iki 2
üç 3
dört 4
beş 5
altı 6
yedi 7
sekiz 8
dokuz 9
on 10
on bir 11
on iki 12
on üç 13
yirmi 20
otuz 30
kırk 40
elli 50
altmış 60
yetmiş 70
seksen 80
doksan 90
yüz 100
yüz kırk 140
iki yüz 200
yedi yüz 700
bin 1000

Food and drink terms

BASICS

bal honey
buz ice
ekmek bread
makarna pasta (noodles)
peynir cheese
pilav, pirinç rice
şeker sugar
su water
süt milk
tereyağı butter
tuz salt
zeytin yağı olive oil
yoğurt yoghurt
yumurta eggs

COOKING TERMS

acı hot, spicy
ezme puréed dip
fırında(n) baked
haşlama stew(ed)
ızgarada(n) grilled
sıcak/soğuk hot/cold (meze)
soslu, salçalı in red sauce
tava, sahanda deep-fried, fried
yoğurtlu in yoghurt sauce
zeytinyağlılar cold cooked vegetables with olive oil
with/without (meat) (et)li/(et)siz

SOUP (ÇORBA)

ezo gelin tomato, rice and lentil
işkembe tripe
mercimek lentil
tarhana yoghurt, grain and spice
tavuk chicken

APPETIZERS (MEZE)

antep or acılı ezmesi spicy tomato/ chilli mash
cacık yoghurt, cucumber and herb dip
çoban salatası tomato, cucumber, parsley, pepper and onion salad
haydarı strained yoghurt and garlic dip
imam bayıldı cold baked aubergine, onion and tomato
mücver courgette fritters
patlıcan ezmesi aubergine pâté

gözleme stuffed paratha-like flatbread
lahmacun flatbread with spicy mincemeat
mantı Turkish "ravioli" in yoghurt sauce
midye dolması rice-stuffed mussels
pide Turkish "pizza"
poğaça soft, often filled, bread roll
simit bread rings studded with sesame seeds

FISH (BALIK) AND SEAFOOD (DENIZ ÜRÜNLERI)

barbunya/tekir red mullet, small/ large
çipura gilt-head bream
hamsi anchovy (Black Sea)
kalamar squid
kalkan turbot
karides prawns
kılıç swordfish
levrek sea bass
lüfer bluefish
mercan pandora/red bream
mezgit whitebait
palamut/torik small/large bonito
sardalya sardine

VEGETABLES (SEBZE)

bamya okra, lady's fingers
biber peppers
domates tomato
ıspanak spinach
kabak courgette
mantar mushrooms
maydanoz parsley
nohut chickpeas
patates potato
patlıcan aubergine
roka, tere rocket greens
salatalık cucumber
soğan onion
taze fasulye French beans

FRUIT (MEYVE) AND NUTS (FISTIK)

antep fıstığı pistachio
badem almond
ceviz walnut

çilek strawberry
elma apple
erik plum
fındık hazlenut
incir fig
karpuz watermelon
kayısı apricot
kiraz sweet cherry
muz banana
nar pomegranate
portakal orange
şeftali peach
üzüm grape

CHEESE

beyaz white goat's cheese, like feta
kaşar yellow cow's cheese
otlu peynir herb-stuffed goat's cheese
tulum goat's cheese cured in a goatskin

SWEETS (TATILAR) AND PASTRIES (PASTALAR)

baklava nut-filled filo pastry
dondurma ice cream
helva sweet made from semolina flour
İrmik helvası semolina and nut helva
kabak tatlısı baked pumpkin served with tahini
kadayıf "shredded wheat" in syrup
lokum Turkish delight
muhallebi milk pudding with rice flour and rosewater
sütlaç rice pudding
tahin helvası sesame paste helva
tavuk göğsü chicken-breast, milk, sugar and rice taffy

DRINKS

ayran drinking yoghurt
bira beer
çay tea
kahve coffee
maden suyu/soda mineral water (fizzy)
meyva suyu fruit juice
şarap wine

Publishing Information
Fourth Edition 2019

Distribution
UK, Ireland and Europe
Apa Publications (UK) Ltd; sales@roughguides.com
United States and Canada
Ingram Publisher Services; ips@ingramcontent.com
Australia and New Zealand
Woodslane; info@woodslane.com.au
Southeast Asia
Apa Publications (SN) Pte; sales@roughguides.com
Worldwide
Apa Publications (UK) Ltd; sales@roughguides.com

Special Sales, Content Licensing and CoPublishing
Rough Guides can be purchased in bulk quantities at discounted prices. We can create special editions, personalised jackets and corporate imprints tailored to your needs. sales@roughguides.com.

roughguides.com
Printed in China by RR Donnelley Asia Printing Solutions Limited

A catalogue record for this book is available from the British Library
The publishers and authors have done their best to ensure the accuracy and currency of all the information in **Pocket Rough Guide Istanbul**, however, they can accept no responsibility for any loss, injury, or inconvenience sustained by any traveller as a result of information or advice contained in the guide.

Rough Guide Credits
Author: Terry Richardson
Updater: Klaudyna Cwynar
Editor: Zara Sekhavati
Cartography: Katie Bennett
Managing editor: Rachel Lawrence
Picture editor: Aude Vauconsant

Cover photo research: Michelle Bhatia
Original design: Richard Czapnik
Senior DTP coordinator: Dan May
Head of DTP and Pre-Press: Rebeka Davies

Help us update

We've gone to a lot of effort to ensure that this edition of the **Pocket Rough Guide Istanbul** is accurate and up-to-date. However, things change – places get "discovered", opening hours are notoriously fickle, restaurants and rooms raise prices or lower standards. If you feel we've got it wrong or left something out, we'd like to know, and if you can remember the address, the price, the hours, the phone number, so much the better.

Please send your comments with the subject line "**Pocket Rough Guide Istanbul Update**" to mail@uk.roughguides.com. We'll credit all contributions and send a copy of the next edition (or any other Rough Guide if you prefer) for the very best emails.

Photo Credits

(Key: T-top; C-centre; B-bottom; L-left; R-right)

Ahmet Gülkokan/Hiç-Contemporary Craftsy 90

Alamy 6, 14B, 18C, 21C, 32, 33, 35, 36, 55, 69, 70, 71, 75, 76, 89, 104, 110, 117, 132/133

Anon 90

Aurora Photos/AWL Images Ltd 2TL

Gavin Hellier/AWL Images Ltd 1

Getty Images 5, 15B, 15T, 19C, 19T, 51, 126

iStock 2BL, 10, 11T, 11B, 16B, 18T, 21T, 31, 34, 43, 88, 100, 127

Lydia Evans/Rough Guides 2CR, 4, 12/13B, 17B, 17T, 18B, 20C, 20T, 30, 37, 38, 40, 41, 48, 52, 56, 59, 64, 65, 66, 67,

73, 80, 81, 83, 85, 93, 95, 101, 103, 105, 106, 109, 116, 119, 121, 123, 124, 131

Murat Germen/Istanbul Modern 13C

Robert Harding 22/23

Roger d'Olivere Mapp/Rough Guides 2BR, 12/13T, 14T, 16T, 19B, 20B, 21C, 25, 47, 54, 63, 77, 99, 113, 129, 142/143

Shutterstock 12B, 82

Turkish Culture and Tourism Office 28

Yiğit Şişmanoğlu/Pixie Underground 111

Cover: Sokollu Mehmet Pasha Mosque
Anna Serrano/4Corners Images

Index

INDEX